OUT FOR A DUCK

Kersi Meher-Homji, born in Bombay and settled in Sydney, is a notable addition to the ranks of Australian cricket writers. A scientist by profession, he has written three cricket books: *Cricket's Great Families* (1980), *1000 Tests* (1984) and *Parsee Cricket Centenary* (1986).

Kersi writes for the *Sydney Morning Herald*, *Cricketer* (Australia), *Inside Edge* (Australia), *Wisden Cricket Monthly* (England), *The Times of India*, *Sportstar* (India) and *Mid Day* (India). He is the sports editor of the *Indian Down Under* — a monthly published in Sydney.

The author comes from a family of cricketers including an uncle who played Test cricket and a grand uncle who toured England in 1911 with an official All India team.

But it is his undoubted skill as a number 11 batsman which is the inspiration behind the book.

'OUT FIRST BALL' (from an original painting by E.P. Kinsella), courtesy Ronald Cardwell

OUT FOR A DUCK

Kersi Meher-Homji
Foreword by Steve Waugh

Kangaroo Press

© Kersi Meher-Homji 1993

First published in 1993 by Kangaroo Press Pty Ltd
3 Whitehall Road Kenthurst NSW 2156 Australia
P.O. Box 6125 Dural Delivery Centre NSW 2158 Australia
Typeset by G.T. Setters Pty Limited
Printed by Griffin Press, Netley, South Australia

ISBN 0 86417 572 8

Contents

No. 23,009

Telephone 20644, Letters to Box 508, GPO, Sydney, 2001.

WEDNESDAY, JANUARY 27, 1982

THE Sun

OVER ONE MILLION READERS'

25 cents'

SUPER VALUE

LIZ BY HER MUM

CHAPPELL DUCKS INTO MORE TROUBLE!

By KEN LAWS and
GEOFF PRENTER

GREG CHAPPELL'S seventh duck added strength last night to persistent speculation he would stand down as captain of the Australian cricket tour to New Zealand.

An angry Chappell faced a press conference last night and said: "I don't feel like standing down now, but who knows how I'll feel next week?"

● Continued Page 2

. . . and Tandberg's View.

Seven ducks . . . Greg Chappell.

12-YEAR-OLD FANS DRUNK ON THE HILL: P2

WHY ARE PEOPLE CRUEL TO HER?

SEE P15

TRAINS: LATE DEAL

STRIKE IS OFF

By MICHAEL PERRY and
JOE BUCHANAN

A STRIKE which would have stopped all trains and Government buses in NSW from midnight was called off this afternoon — only minutes before the strike deadline.

● Continued Page 2

---

80 PAGES TODAY ● WEATHER: Mild days (Map P57). ● LOTTERY: Opera House 751, P56. ● FINANCE: P72. ● TV: P36.

Foreword

It happened four years ago but I recall it as if it was yesterday.

It felt great winning all those Tests and scoring all those runs in the 1989 Ashes series in England. Previously, many had doubted my ever hitting a Test century, so it was nice to average over 125 in a six-Test series against the traditional enemy.

I had just returned from this successful but tiring tour and was resting when a nervous voice on the phone requested me to write a foreword for his book on cricket. It was the first time anyone had asked me to do a foreword and I was naturally curious. Would it be a coaching manual or a biography, I wondered. I was brought down to earth when told that the book was all about ducks and pairs.

A book on ducks? How perverse, I thought! I had forgotten all about it till Kersi Meher-Homji sent me the manuscript recently. I realised that research on cricket — especially on a *Wisden*-neglected topic like zeros — takes an awfully long time to prepare. To my surprise, I found his manuscript a good read; interesting, relaxing, in parts amusing and totally engrossing.

And consoling, too. Far from poking fun at the ducksters, the book includes thought-provoking chapters: It happens to the Best and There *is* Life after Ducks. We have all heard about Sir Donald Bradman's duck in his final Test innings at The Oval in 1948 but I did not know that he made 16 ducks in his first-class career — six of them off the first ball!

Nor did I realise that Sir Len Hutton had started both his first-class and Test careers with noughts.

More in my generation, Greg Chappell failed to score five times in seven internationals in 1981–82, chronicles Kersi.

And I thought life was unbearable when adjudged lbw to Iqbal Qasim for a duck in the Karachi Test of September 1988. This was the third duck of my Test career; the previous ones were both registered on the SCG: against India in 1986 and England a year later. I still remember the pangs.

A duck is a leveller. After two unbeaten hundreds at Headingley and Lord's and a 92 at Old Trafford way back in 1989, I started my innings in the Trent Bridge Test with confidence. And why not? The score was 4–543 and my series average a hot 242.50. But soon I was back in the dressing room — c. Gower, b. Malcolm for a nought.

Out for a Duck neither ridicules the ducksters nor does it try to glorify their non-deeds. Kersi quotes Dr W.G. Grace: 'A player could not call himself a cricketer until he'd been out for a duck'. And who should know more about the ups and downs of cricket than myself after the sobering 1990–91 and 1991–92 seasons?

Not that this book is all about non-achievements. It highlights the feats of Arthur Morris and Bill Lawry who avoided the dreaded 'Daddles' in their first 100 first-class innings. Also despite all his recent misfortunes, David Gower evaded a duck in 119 Test innings. Kersi also chronicles that Sir Richard Hadlee dismissed most batsman, 66, for ducks in Test cricket and Imran has claimed 62 Test ducksters. Just as well they have retired!

However, another one of Kersi's statistics frankly worries me. Kapil Dev, he writes, has dismissed 65 batsmen for ducks in the Test arena. I hope he never adds me to his collection!

Stephen Waugh
May 1993

Acknowledgments

I would like to thank Stephen Waugh for his inspiring Foreword; Ross Dundas for checking some of the figures, suggesting changes and for his valuable help; Ronald Cardwell for providing a few unpublished photographs and on research on the Primary Club of Australia; Allan Miller for his invaluable assistance and encouragement; Jack Pollard for the use of rare pictures and for his constant support; Carl Harrison-Ford for his editorial expertise; librarians Cliff Winning (N.S.W. Cricket Association Library) and Stephen Gibbs for unearthing some rare references; Ken Piesse, Rusi Surti and John Benaud for the supply of pictures; Philip Bailey for allowing the use of his research on ducks in a row; and Anadji Dossa, Bapoo Mama, Dr Vasant Naik, Atul Kahate, Malcolm Burns and Jack Brown for providing and checking some of the data.

The following authors are quoted: Ray Robinson from *From the Boundary*, (Collins, 1950); Basil Easterbrook and R.C. Robertson-Glasgow from *Wisden* 1971; Irving Rosenwater from *Cricket Quarterly Facts and Figures*, (Vol.2 No 4, 1975); Gerald Brodribb from *All Round the Wicket* (Sporting Handbooks, 1951); Jonathan Rice from *Wisden Cricket Monthly* (June 1987); Greg Growden from the *Sydney Morning Herald*; Jack Egan from *Extra Cover*, (Pan Books, 1989); Dudley Nourse from *Cricket in the Blood*, (Hodder & Stoughton, 1949); and Julian Oakley from *Cricket Companion '74* (Australia Cricket Society, ACT, 1974).

Books and periodicals to which I have referred include: *The Wisden Book of Cricket Records* by Bill Frindall; *Wisden*

Cricketers' Almanack (several issues); *The Cricket Statistician,* (Autumn 1986); *This Curious Game of Cricket* by George Mell (Unwin Paperbacks, 1982); *Ranji—A Century Album* edited by Vasant Raiji (Seven Star Publications, 1972); *First Class Cricket in Australia,* Vol 1, 1850–51 to 1941–42 by Ray Webster and Allan Miller (Webster, 1991); *Figures on the Green* by Derek Lodge (George Allen & Unwin, 1982); *The Gillette Book of Cricket and Football* edited by Gordon Ross (1963); *The Cricketer Book of Cricket Disasters and Bizarre Records* by C.D.A. Martin-Jenkins (Century Publishing, 1983); *The Cricketer Book of Cricket Eccentrics* by C.D.A. Martin-Jenkins (Century Publishing, 1985); *Cricketer* (Australia) edited by Ken Piesse (several issues); *100 Summers* edited by Ken Piesse (Newspress Pty Ltd, 1982); *Wisden Cricket Monthly* edited by David Frith (several issues); *Australian Cricket* edited by Jack Pollard (Hodder & Stoughton, 1982); *The Primary Club's Middle and Leg* edited by Jack Pollard (Macmillan, 1988); *Sportsweek* (India) edited by Khalid Ansari; *Hill Chatter* a publication of the Sydney branch of the Australian Cricket Society 1974; and the *Daily Mirror* (Sydney).

Cartoons are from: *The Sun* (Sydney); and *The West Australian.* I also thank cartoonists John Shakespeare, Tony Rafty and Shane Leahy for their original artwork.

Some of the pictures are reproduced courtesy *Cricketer* magazine (Australia), *Wisden Cricket Monthly* (England), the *Sydney Morning Herald, The Age* (Melbourne) and *Herald-Sun* (Melbourne).

An elite rabbit was Albert Wright of South Australia. He started his first-class career in 1905–06 with six ducks—still a record. (Jack Pollard collection)

Introduction

For once I started a book without any self-doubt. It is easy writing reams on triple centurions and bowlers bagging seven wickets in an innings, but you feel edgy when a reader confronts you with: 'Now tell me, how many centuries did you score?' or 'Bet you took a few hat tricks in your time'.

And when I blurt out, 'Er, my highest score is 42 and, um... I was known more as an off-line rather than an off-spin bowler', my credibility sinks.

However, no-one can doubt my expertise when it comes to scoring ducks. I am up there (or is it down there?) with the best, rubbing shoulders with those real zero champs — characters like Northamptonshire's B.J. Griffith who once scored 10 zeros in a row in eight matches; Victoria's Jimmy Higgs (who completed the 1975 tour of England without a run against his name); and India's B.S. Chandrasekhar who turned non-scoring into a fine art.

My eyes twinkle when asked: 'So you have scored more ducks than runs. Which was your most important duck?'

No ers and ums now. No pondering deeply. The reply comes fast and almost with a touch of arrogance. It was at Bombay's Dadar Union Gymkhana where all-time greats Ajit Wadekar, Sunil Gavaskar and Dilip Vengsarkar learnt their cricket. It happened in a low division Kanga League match in 1968. Two of my team mates were out off successive balls and I was the next man in.

On a hat trick and I could barely contain myself. As if the opposition was unaware of this, I informed the bowler, the wicket-keeper and the umpires. Came the magic moment; a straight ball which I attempted to play back. It kept low and hit me on the pads.

Up went the umpire's finger and my spirit.

That was the most important duck of my career. The players and both the umpires gathered around, congratulating both me and the bowler. Pity, my captain did not join in the celebration and refused to shake my outstretched hand when I returned to the tent.

If you had asked Sir Leonard Hutton as to his best Test innings, he may have ranked his 62 not out on a 'sticky' wicket in the Brisbane Test of December 1950 ahead of his 19 centuries (even including his 364 against Australia at The Oval in 1938). Technically, my best low score was also not a duck.

It was at the Gosford Oval, New South Wales, in 1974, the first ever match played by the Sydney branch of the Australian Cricket Society. Against a local team full of Davidsons, all related to the great all-rounder Alan Davidson, I was bowled first ball but the umpire called it a no-ball. I snicked the next delivery which the wicket-keeper dropped. The next three balls beat my bat and stumps very, very narrowly.

At the other end was Alan Crompton, then Sydney University's first grade wicket-keeper batsman, later Australia's manager for tours to New Zealand and India and currently the chairman of the Australian Cricket Board. He shielded me for some 20 minutes. But after six more chances, I mistimed a snick to a nicety and it became — lo and behold! — a cover drive. As I stood stunned, Crompton at my end whispered: 'Great shot, but stop admiring and start running'. We ran three.

If ever a batsman deserved a perfect duck I did that day, but I was foiled by good luck. In sharp contrast, the great Ranjitsinhji in the early 1900s had a shattering experience. For Gentlemen v Players, he received nine deliveries and he played aggressive shots to all of them, but agile fielding prevented what would have been fours. He was brilliantly caught off the ninth ball, which he later insisted he had played correctly.

In his farewell Test at Birmingham in July 1990, Sir Richard Hadlee brought ducks on to the front page of newspapers just as Sir Donald Bradman had done in his Test farewell at The Oval in 1948. When Hadlee bowled England's Devon Malcolm for a duck in the first innings, he had claimed his 63rd Test duck — a record. Before this the record was shared by Pakistani captain Imran Khan and himself.

Inspired, the Kiwi knight 'shot' three more ducks in the second innings, 'Jack' Russell, Eddie Hemmings and the unfortunate Malcolm (who got a pair). Dramatically, Hadlee had claimed a pair — Malcolm's double scalp — with his last ball in Test cricket.

Pairs once again made headlines in the 1992–93 season when Mark Waugh made two pairs in successive Tests against Sri Lanka, and Keith Arthurton and Ian Healy registered a pair each in the thrilling Adelaide Test. And when Allan Border — on the verge of overtaking Sunil Gavaskar's Test aggregate record — made a nought and a nought in Perth, the *Sydney Morning Herald* headlined the story on the front page: 'DOUBLE DUCKS. Our Heroic Failures'.

The book does not claim to be an encyclopaedia on ducks — what could be more boring? At Test level I have been thorough and have given figures *Wisden* has failed to. But at first-class and more so at minor cricket levels, I have presented interesting rather than exhaustive records. Throughout the book, I have emphasised drama, humour, heartbreak and bizarre happenings involved in the making of a duck.

1 Starting at T'bottom

They have to be picked out, like a few pearls from
legions of oysters.

— R.C. Robertson-Glasgow

'They' are cricket's ugly ducklings with more aliases than the
Great Train Robber. Call them ducks, blobs, noughts, no-
scores, zilch, zoinks, blongers, full moon, glozzers, globes,
cyphers, eggs, potatoes, a pair of spectacles or a brace (for
a twin act), 'Daddles' or zeros — they sound equally
depressing and unappetising to batsmen.

'Making a duck's egg' was a term coined in the 1860s
because the figure '0' resembles a duck's egg. Later some
scoreboard owners with a sense of humour put on the
scoreboard an actual drawing of a duck instead of the dismal
figure '0'. In fact, a duck is the only score a cricketer can
make which has become symbolised. The legend started when
0's resemblance to a duck's egg first prompted a rural
barracker to quack at a blushing batsman. Since that day
a score of 0 became an 'emblem of futility', according to the
doyen of Australian cricket writers, Ray Robinson.

Colonial archives record that one Frederick McEnvoy of
Melbourne Town played Major B.J. Wardell a single-wicket
match for 12 dinners in the 1890s. Each was allowed three
fielders and one of the umpires was Australia's Test captain,
Harry Trott. McEnvoy won the toss and scored 34. He
dismissed Wardell twice for no score, for which he received
two eggs from Trott. The major retaliated by smashing them
on his head.

A duck provokes different reactions among spectators, ranging from sympathy to laughter. At times it is like something out of a Laurel and Hardy movie. And that is why 'Daddle Duck' — a 1970s invention of PBL marketing and Channel 9, Australia — received wild cheering every time he walked, sad or furious, with the duckster back to the pavilion.

A duckster may pretend to laugh about it or be philosophical about it, but it is a traumatic experience. Like finding your brand new car stolen or your reproductive organs removed. The tragedy is intensified when you fail to score in your first big match. But all is not lost if 'Daddles' follows your first such outing. Many famous batsmen have started their career this way only to scale heights later on.

Few among us know that the great Len Hutton (6,971 runs in 79 Tests, average 56.67 and 40,140 first-class runs at 55.51) started as a 'zero champion'. He scored a duck in his first innings for Yorkshire seconds, a duck for Yorkshire (at Fenners in 1934) and a duck in his first Test innings against New Zealand at Lord's on 26 June 1937. In the second innings of that Test, he scored a single — so it was very nearly a pair. Fortunately, he was picked in the next Test at Old Trafford where he made 100 and 14 and never looked back.

In the Lord's match, Hutton's opening partner, J.H. Parks, also made his Test debut and scored 22 and 7. He was dropped in the next Test and was never selected again. 'Oh why didn't I score a duck?' could well have been his lament. In the same Test, another great batsman, Martin Donnelly, made his Test debut for New Zealand and scored a nought.

When Hutton failed to break his duck in his county debut, Maurice Leyland consoled him in his strong Yorkshire brogue: 'Never mind Leonard, tha's started at t'bottom'. Incidentally, Leyland himself had scored a duck in his Test debut in 1928.

Despite the shaky start, Hutton ended on top, climaxed by being one of the few players knighted for his cricketing ability. Among other great players to make ducks in their Test debut were Victor Trumper, the Trott brothers, Joe Darling, the three Gregorys, Majid Khan and Graham Gooch.

The great Middlesex and English batsman, Patsy Hendren, started and finished his first-class career with ducks. In between, however, he amassed 57,611 runs (only Jack Hobbs and Frank Woolley have scored more) and hit 170 centuries (only Jack Hobbs ahead of him).

The Gregory clan which dominated the Australian Test scene from 1877 to 1929 was also painfully aware of the 'starting at t'bottom' feeling. Edward Gregory, brother of Dave who captained Australia in the inaugural Test of 1877, his son Syd and Syd's cousin Jack, all scored ducks in their Test debut. Far from being deterred they went on to score 3,439 runs between them in 83 Tests, hitting six hundreds and 15 fifties. Jack's century in 70 minutes against South Africa at Johannesburg in 1921–22 remains one Test record Viv Richards or Ian Botham has failed to better in hurricane hitting. India's consistent batsman, Dilip Vengsarkar (6,868 runs from 116 Tests) also started his first-class career with a duck in 1975–76. After years of waiting, Zimbabwe-born Graeme Hick made an inauspicious Test debut against West Indies in 1991. The 'White Hope' (with thousands of runs in County cricket) could average only 10.71 in the series (with ducks in his second and third Test) before being dropped.

G.F. Grace had the unpleasant experience of recording the first pair in Test history. This was in the first ever Test on English soil against Australia at The Oval in 1880. As this was his only Test match — he died a month later — he had bagged a pair in his first and only Test. Others in this unenviable group are C.D. Dixon, P.T. Lewis, P.S. Twentyman-Jones and C.S. Wimble of South Africa, L.A. Butterfield and C.G. Rowe of New Zealand, Rashid Patel of India and Pakistan's Saeed Anwar. England's opening batsman, Graham Gooch, bagged a pair in his Test debut in 1975 but soon overcame this horror start and has recorded several Test tons — climaxing it by recording 333, 123 and 116 in successive Test innings against India in 1990.

In all, 25 batsman have registered pairs in their Test debut, K.R. Rutherford of New Zealand and Pakistan's Saeed Anwar

being the only opening batsmen to do so. They are listed in
Appendix II.

J.T. Willoughby was the first player to be selected again
after a debut pair. He was dismissed in both innings by
George Lohmann but retaliated by sending back his
tormentor for a pair as well.

In the Christchurch Test of 1929–30, the inaugural Test for
New Zealand, Ken James and Fred Badcock were the victims
of M.J.C. Allom in the course of his hat trick in the first innings.

Four players have started their Test careers with three ducks.
They are Tommy Ward of South Africa in 1912, Bob Massie
of Australia in 1972, New Zealander Brendon Bracewell in
1978 and Australian Merv Hughes from 1985–86 to 1986–87.
C.R. Rangachari of India began his Test career against
Australia in 1947–48 with 0*,0,0,0* and 0.

Their disappointing starts could be the inspiration behind
this anonymous verse reprinted in D.M. Woodhead's *Three
Ducks on the Trot*:

> Three ducks on the trot,
> Or merely a pair,
> Dear batsman, is not
> An excuse for despair
> But a signal for laughter;
> Your century comes after.

None of these four got a century later, although Ward did
manage 64 in the Johannesburg Test of 1922–23 and 50 in
the Old Trafford Test. His end was tragic. He was electrocuted
while working in a goldmine before he was 50. Merv Hughes
was luckier. In successive Tests in 1989 he surprised everyone
by hitting 72 not out at Adelaide against the mighty West
Indies and 71 against England at Leeds. In the early 1990s
he has improved his batting to an extent that prompted
skipper Border to comment tongue-in-cheek, 'Hughes can
be called an all-rounder, if only he can take some wickets!'

The spectacular effort of a duck is amplified when an

opening batsman is dismissed without scoring in the first over
of a Test match. The silence from a 30,000 strong home crowd
is almost deafening. India's bespectacled opener Pankaj Roy
was a prolific duckster, recording 14 noughts in 75 completed
Test innings. He had a nighmarish Test series in England in
1952 when against Fred Trueman and Alec Bedser he failed
to score five times out of eight — four times in a row
including a pair in the Old Trafford Test.

However, once he broke the duck barrier, he carried on
smoothly; 2,442 runs in 43 Tests at 32.56, reaching centuries
five times and fifties nine times. In the Madras Test of
1955–56 against New Zealand, Roy (173) added 413 runs for
the first wicket with Vinoo Mankad (231), a world record
which still stands. So there is life after ducks after all.

More dramatic than an opener making a duck is both the
openers failing to score. In Test cricket there are so far 27
instances of both opening batsmen recording noughts. They
are:

Openers	Team	Opponent	Venue	Series
P.S. McDonnell & A.C. Bannerman	Australia	England	Manchester	1888
G. Challenor & C.A. Roach	West Indies	England	Manchester	1928
H. Sutcliffe & E. Paynter	England	New Zealand	Christchurch	1932–33
J.H.W. Fingleton & C.L. Badcock	Australia	England	Bridgetown	1936–37
W.J. O'Reilly & L.O'B. Fleetwood-Smith	Australia	England	Melbourne	1936–37
A.R. Morris & J. Moroney	Australia	South Africa	Johannesburg	1949–50
J. Moroney & A.R. Morris	Australia	England	Brisbane	1950–51
Pankaj Roy & D.K. Gaekwad	India	England	Leeds	1952
D.J. McGlew & T.L. Goddard	South Africa	England	Lord's	1955
C.C. Hunte & R.B. Kanhai	West Indies	Pakistan	Port-of-Spain	1957–58
J.K. Holt & C.C. Hunte	West Indies	India	Kanpur	1958–59

Openers	Team	Opponent	Venue	Series
S.N. McGregor &				
G.T. Dowling	New Zealand	South Africa	Johannesburg	1961-62
M.L. Jaisimha &				
K.S. Indrajitsinhji	India	Australia	Madras	1964-65
T.W. Jarvis &				
M.J.F. Shrimpton	New Zealand	England	Auckland	1965-66
M.H. Denness &				
D.L. Amiss	England	Pakistan	Hyderabad	1972-73
S.M. Gavaskar &				
C.P.S. Chauhan	India	Australia	Melbourne	1977-78
A.E. Greenidge &				
A.B. Williams	West Indies	India	Bombay	1978-79
D.W. Randall & G. Boycott	England	Australia	Perth	1979-80
Shafiq Ahmed &				
Sadiq Mohammad[a]	Pakistan	West Indies	Karachi	1980-81
Mudassar Nazar &				
Rizwan-uz-Zaman	Pakistan	Australia	Perth	1981-82
Mohsin Khan &				
Mudassar Nazar	Pakistan	England	Leeds	1982
C.G. Greenidge &				
D.L. Haynes	West Indies	India	Port-of-Spain	1982-83
S. Wettimuny &				
E.R.N.S. Fernando	Sri Lanka	Australia	Kandy	1982-83
G.A. Gooch &				
R.T. Robinson	England	West Indies	Kingston	1985-86
J.G. Wright & B.A. Edgar	New Zealand	England	Lord's	1986
J.G. Wright &				
B.R. Hartland	New Zealand	England	Auckland	1991-92
Saheed Ahmed &				
Rameez Raja	Pakistan	West Indies	St John's	1992-93

[a] Both openers were out lbw to Sylvester Clarke. Coincidentally, in this Test the numbers 10 and 11 (Iqbal Qasim and Nazir jnr) also made ducks. In all, six ducks were recorded in this innings — which is a record for maximum noughts in a Test innings.

Arthur Morris and Jack Moroney represent the only openers to experience this double disaster twice. Their first such experience against South Africa in the first Test at Johannesburg in 1949–50 was remarkable for both. Before this Test, Morris had played 101 first-class innings without making a duck and it had to happen in a Test match. On the other hand, it was Moroney's Test debut and he was run out.

In the fourth Test of the series against practically the same attack and on the same ground, Morris and Moroney recaptured their form adding 214 for the opening wicket and each registered centuries. Moroney went on to score an unbeaten 101 in the second innings, becoming the only Australian to hit two centuries in a Test against the Springboks.

However, it seems to be hundreds or nothings for these openings M's of Australian cricket. In the first Test at Brisbane the following summer, Moroney made a pair. In the second innings both Moroney and Morris made ducks and, with Sam Loxton joining in the act, Australia was at one stage three down for nought. It was a typical Brisbane 'sticky' and Australia declared at 7–32 but still won by 70 runs.

Australia's record low start of 3 for 0 was shattered 18 months later when India in the Leeds Test of 1952 lost her first four batsmen — Pankaj Roy, Dattaji Gaekwad, Madhav Mantri and Vijay Manjrekar — without a run on the board. This was due to the English fast bowler Fred Trueman, who on his Test debut secured three of these wickets in eight balls.

Do ducks run in the family? Ask Norm O'Neill and his son Mark. Norm O'Neill, before he got the Bradmanesque tag, made his Sheffield Shield debut for New South Wales against South Australia at the Adelaide Oval in 1959. He was out second ball. Twenty years on, on 27 October 1979, Mark also scored a duck in his Sheffield Shield debut for Western Australia v New South Wales on the SCG — bowled second ball by Len Pascoe. From Perth, Norm sent a cable to him saying 'I know how you feel. It was my off-stump too. You were not good enough today but tomorrow is another day.'

Sure enough, two days later Mark O'Neill scored a polished 52 in the second innings. However, in 1991 he had the misfortune of making four ducks in a row for New South Wales in Sheffield Shield — climaxing with a pair in the Final against Victoria in Melbourne.

If you are looking for a real life tear-jerker, few television soapies can match the trauma and tragedy of Dr Roy Park, the popular Victorian batsman. Born on 30 July 1892 in Ballarat, Victoria, 17 year-old Roy first drew attention when he headed the batting average for Melbourne Cricket Club while still a student at Wesley College. After scoring a century in a Sheffield Shield match against South Australia when 21, he was picked to tour South Africa in 1914. Due to the outbreak of World War I the tour was cancelled.

The war only delayed his progress for he came back with a string of hundreds (five centuries and a double century) in Shield matches. Then the glorious moment; he was selected to represent Australia in the second Test against England on his home ground, Melbourne, in 1920–21.

Warwick Armstrong won the toss and Australia batted. After Herbie Collins and Warren Bardsley had put on 116 runs for the opening wicket, the next man in was local boy and debutant Roy Park. The large first day crowd stood and cheered their popular batsman all the way from the pavilion to the wicket. It was one of the finest receptions ever accorded a batsman, for his home crowd loved and admired the doctor.

As he got ready to play his first ball in Test cricket from the Warwickshire medium pacer, Harry Howell, a hush descended around the ground. Park played the stroke but deflected the ball on to his wicket and was bowled first ball. Perhaps the reception as he walked out was too overwhelming for him. He walked back slowly in silence to be swallowed up in eternal darkness as far as Test cricket was concerned. Australia scored 499, won this Test by an innings and 91 runs, and Roy sadly was never picked again to represent his country.

His strongest supporter, his wife, was present that day before his entry, knitting intensely to battle her nerves. As Howell ran in to deliver the fateful ball she dropped her ball of knitting wool, bent down to retrieve it and when she

Tragedy dark and true. Victoria's favourite batsman and doctor, Roy Park, played only one Test innings (on MCG 1920–21) and was bowled first ball. (Jack Pollard collection)

surfaced she had missed what eventually turned out to be her husband's entire Test batting career!

Pity there was no instant replay on the scoreboard those days. In a way it was just as well for the sight of 'Daddles Duck' following a lonely, dejected Roy would have added to Mrs Park's heartbreak.

The Test tragedy notwithstanding, Roy Park's cricket career was quite successful. He scored 2,514 runs in first-class cricket (including a century for Victoria against England in March 1923) at an average of 40.50. His daughter, Lal, married off-spinner Ian Johnson who played 45 Tests, 17 times as Australia's captain.

But in the New Year Test of 1947 against England, Johnson suffered a calamity which may have reminded him of his father-in-law's fate 26 years previously. In the Melbourne Test, Johnson was out lbw first ball and had five days to brood about it before he got a chance in the second innings. On the rest day, Lindsay Hassett, that loveable humorist, invited the Johnson family to Sunday dinner and served them a couple of ducks. Johnson refused politely and firmly, gorging only on the vegetables and dessert. Not that it helped. Next morning, in his eagerness to avoid the pair, he went for a suicidal single and ran himself out.

2 It Happens to the Best

If all the best players in cricket were good
enough to avoid ever getting a duck, what a
boring game cricket would be.
                                    — Irving Rosenwater

You have really established yourself as a batsman when your
duck makes headlines. Sir Donald Bradman's duck in his final
Test innings against England at The Oval in 1948 made front-
page news. And the emotional drama of the event is still
remembered even more than some of his big scores.

For a prolific run-getter like Bradman to score ducks is
a great pacifier. If Bradman can make seven ducks in 80 Test
innings, a mere mortal is allowed his share of failures without
feeling guilty or despondent. In first-class cricket, Bradman
failed to score on 16 occasions, which represent more than
any other individual score against his name.

To record a zero was so rare for Dr W.G. Grace that Punch
magazine in 1884 composed a poem to commemorate his
duck off Fred Spofforth:

> Our Grace before dinner was very soon done,
> And Grace after dinner did not get a run.

A duck could be majestic as well as embarrassing and
frustrating. Although the great Ranji never bagged a pair in
his 500 first-class innings, he loved to talk about his famous
duck. To quote his equally illustrious nephew Duleepsinhji:

Dr W.G. Grace: 'A player could not call himself a cricketer until he'd been out for a duck.' (Ronald Cardwell collection)

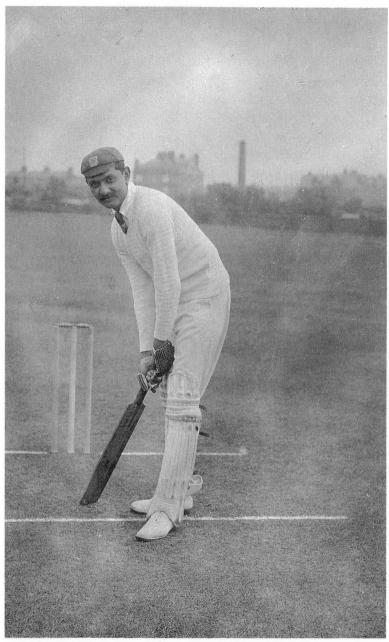

K.S. Ranjitsinhji, the touch artist, had nodding acquaintance with ducks but never made a pair. (Ronald Cardwell collection)

'The only innings of which Uncle spoke to me was a duck in a Gentlemen v Players match. He said he received nine balls and he played a good shot to each of them. But in each case brilliant fielding prevented what would have been a boundary. He was brilliantly caught off the ninth ball which he said he had played correctly.'

J.W.H.T. ('Johnny Won't Hit Today') Douglas, a recognised batsman, made 94 ducks in first-class cricket while the elegant Frank Woolley made 89 in 1,532 innings. Woolley's most non-productive match was for Kent v Lancashire in 1909 when he bagged a pair, took no catches or wickets and bowled no maidens in 18 frustrating overs.

Apart from Ranji, other all time great batsmen — W.G. Grace, Sir Jack Hobbs, Bradman, Herbert Sutcliffe, Herbie Taylor, Duleep, Warren Bardsley, Charlie Macartney and Denis Compton never registered pairs. However, equally great names like Wally Hammond and Patsy Hendren collected four pairs each and Philip Mead three in first-class cricket. At Test level, well-known batsmen have bagged pairs — namely Victor Trumper, Frank Worrell, Everton Weekes, Gordon Greenidge, Vijay Hazare, Dilip Vengsarkar, Mohinder Amarnath (twice), Graham Gooch (on debut), Ian Botham, Dennis Amiss, Kim Hughes, Allan Border, Mark Waugh (in successive Tests) not to forget Monty Noble and Syd Gregory recording joint pairs in the Leeds Test of 1899 and Neil Harvey and Ken Mackay in the 1956 'Laker's Test' at Old Trafford, Manchester.

To a top class batsman — and his fans — the only thing in the world more depressing and humiliating than a pair is a King Pair; being dismissed first ball in both innings. This has happened to established batsmen in first-class cricket. Some striking examples include:

Batsman	Team	Opponent	Venue	Season
A. Hearne	Kent	Surrey	The Oval	1894
F.H. Sugg	Lancashire	Essex	Manchester	1897
W. Newham	Sussex	Surrey	Brighton	1898

Jack Hobbs, the champion batsman with most centuries (197) and most runs (61,237) in first-class cricket, made 42 ducks but avoided a pair. (Ronald Cardwell collection)

Batsman	Team	Opponent	Venue	Season
A.E.R. Gilligan	Sussex	Cambridge Uni	Cambridge	1922
A.W. Carr	Nottinghamshire	Essex	Nottingham	1927
C. Wesley	South Africa	England	Nottingham	1960

'Duck fever' is universal and hits you when you least expect it. Greg Chappell had a massive dose of it in 1981–82 when he scored seven ducks in 15 internationals, including four ducks in a row. It was all quite inexplicable because the Australian skipper had started the season confidently with a dazzling 162 (two sixes and twenty fours) in the opening match for Queensland against Pakistan, followed by a brilliant 201 in the Brisbane Test (also off Imran and Sarfraz) the same month.

It was run-scoring business as usual for one of the most consistent postwar batsmen. Or so it seemed. But soon the wheels started falling off. Here is how he struggled in successive internationals from 15 December 1981 to 26 January 1982:

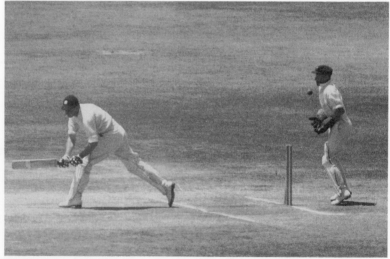

Wally Hammond hears the 'death rattle'. Despite all his consistency, the master batsman made 49 ducks including four pairs in first-class cricket. (Ronald Cardwell collection)

Date	Opponent	Match	Score
15 December 1981	Pakistan	Melbourne Test, second innings	0
17 December 1981	Pakistan	Sydney, Limited Over International	0
20 December 1981	West Indies	Perth, Limited Over International	0 *
26 December 1981	West Indies	Melbourne Test, first innings	0 *
28 December 1981	West Indies	Melbourne Test, second innings	6
3 January 1982	West Indies	Sydney Test, first innings	12
6 January 1982	West Indies	Sydney Test, second innings	0 *
9 January 1982	Pakistan	Melbourne, Limited Over International	35
10 January 1982	West Indies	Melbourne, Limited Over International	59
14 January 1982	Pakistan	Sydney, Limited Over International	36
17 January 1982	West Indies	Brisbane, Limited Over International	61
19 January 1982	West Indies	Sydney, Limited Over International	0
23 January 1982	West Indies	Melbourne, Limited Over International	4
24 January 1982	West Indies	Melbourne, Limited Over International	1
26 January 1982	West Indies	Sydney, Limited Over International	0

* First ball

Thus in 15 consecutive innings (including five innings in three Tests) Chappell had struggled to make 214 runs at 14.26 with two fifties (a highest score of 61) and seven ducks. He was out first ball three times, twice in Test matches.

In five successive Test innings within 23 days (from 15 December 1981 to 6 January 1982) he made 0,0,6,12 and 0, in all 18 runs at 3.60. To extend the sequence a little further, Australia had also played the final Test against India at MCG the previous season. In the second innings, on 10 February 1981, Chappell was out first ball. Thus in one calendar year, 1981, he had scored three ducks in three Melbourne Tests; 76 and 0 v India, 22 and 0 v Pakistan, and 0 and 6 v West Indies.

Cartoonists had a field day depicting Chappell's plight and a poster on the first day of the Sydney Test in January 1982 read: 'Everyone got turkey for Christmas, our Greg got four ducks'.

Chappell recovered his form sufficiently in New Zealand with a masterly 176 in the Christchurch Test two months later.

And in his final Test appearance, against Pakistan at Sydney, he scored a majestic 182, overtaking Bradman's Test aggregate of 6,996 runs and becoming Australia's first batsman to top 7,000 Test runs. The frightful summer of 1981–82 was now a dim memory.

Greg Chappell's successor as Australian captain, Kim Hughes, had a nightmarish summer in 1984–85. Against the all-conquering West Indies he led Australia to two shattering defeats: his personal contributions being 4 and 3, 34 and 4. This led to his resignation after an emotional press conference. He played the next two Tests under Allan Border but his form further deteriorated, scoring a first-ball duck and 2 at Adelaide and a pair at Melbourne, dismissed first ball in the second innings.

Selected in two Benson and Hedges World Championship matches, he scored a duck against England and one against Pakistan — both on the MCG. He led the Rebel Australians to South Africa in 1985–86 and 1986–87 without quite

Kim Hughes is run out for a duck against India on the MCG in 1981. Worse was to befall him in 1984 when he said a sad farewell to Test cricket with a pair on the same ground. (*Herald-Sun*, Melbourne)

recapturing his glory of earlier days. The third unofficial Test against South Africa at Johannesburg in 1985–86 was traumatic for Kim, dismissed first ball in both innings. Then going in as Rodney Hogg's runner he was run out first ball. So he went to the middle three times in one match and returned all three times first ball. This was more than a King Pair — perhaps an Emperor Pair?

India's reliable middle order batsman Mohinder Amarnath experienced an amazing twist of fortunes in Test arena from 12 December 1982 to 14 December 1983. In the first six months against Imran Khan (in Pakistan) and against Joel Garner, Malcolm Marshall, Michael Holding and Andy Roberts (in the West Indies) he plundered 1,182 runs at 69.53 in 11 Tests with five centuries and seven fifties.

As India's vice-captain in the Prudential Cup of 1983, he was adjudged 'Man of the Match' in the semi-final against England and in the final against West Indies as India shocked the world to lift the Cup. His tumble started on home wickets.

After 4 and 7 in two Tests against Pakistan, he had a horror series against West Indies: 0 and 0 at Kanpur, 1 and 0 at Delhi, and 0 and 0 at Calcutta; just one run in the series at an average of 0.17.

The same attack he had earlier punished to top-score in the series in Caribbean, making 598 runs at 66.44 with two centuries and four fifties. But like Greg Chappell before him, Amarnath soon regained his form and became among the more consistent run-getters.

Fifteen batsmen have been dismissed by the first ball of a Test on 17 occasions. Ironically, the only batsmen to suffer more than one such 'nightmare return' is the champion run getter, Sunil Gavaskar. He went through such a sobering experience thrice — in 1974 (v England, Birmingham), in 1983–84 (v West Indies at Calcutta) and in 1986–87 (v Pakistan at Jaipur).

And the only bowlers to serve such drastic departure notice twice are England's Geoff Arnold, New Zealand great Richard Hadlee and India's Kapil Dev.

DISMISSED BY THE FIRST BALL OF A TEST

Batsman	Team	Opponent	Venuue	Series	Bowler
A.C. MacLaren	England	Australia	Melbourne	1894-95	A. Conningham
T.W. Hayward	England	South Africa	The Oval	1907	A.E.E. Vogler
W. Bardsley	Australia	England	Leeds	1926	M.W. Tate
H. Sutcliffe	England	New Zealand	Christchurch	1932-33	F.T. Badcock
T.S. Worthington	England	Australia	Brisbane	1936-37	E.L. McCormick
C.C. Hunte	West Indies	Pakistan	Port-of-Spain	1957-58	Fazal Mahmood
E.J. Barlow	South Africa	Australia	Durban	1966-67	G.D. McKenzie
R.C. Fredericks	West Indies	India	Port-of-Spain	1970-71	S. Abid Ali
K.R. Stackpole	Australia	New Zealand	Auckland	1973-74	R.J. Hadlee
S.M. Gavaskar	India	England	Birmingham	1974	G.G. Arnold
S.S. Naik	India	West Indies	Calcutta	1974-75	A.M.E. Roberts
J.F.M. Morrison	New Zealand	England	Christchurch	1974-75	G.G. Arnold
Mohsin Khan	Pakistan	India	Jullundur(a)	1983-84	Kapil Dev
S.M. Gavaskar	India	West Indies	Calcutta	1983-84	M.D. Marshall
S.M. Gavaskar	India	Pakistan	Jaipur(a)	1986-87	Imran Khan
W.V. Raman	India	New Zealand	Napier	1989-90	R.J. Hadlee
S.J. Cook(b)	South Africa	India	Durban	1992-93	Kapil Dev

(a) It was the first ball ever bowled on this venue.
(b) It was Cook's Test debut.

Very few have evaded a duck in a career of 40 or more Test innings; a couple of instances to leap to one's mind are Australia's Jim Burke (44 Test innings without a nought) and Reggie Duff (40 zeroless innings). But their Test careers were relatively short.

The former West Indies captain, Clive Lloyd, holds the record of playing maximum Test innings, 58, before his first duck. His duck-free career lasted from 1966–67 to 1973–74. He is followed by team-mate Basil Butcher and Australian greats Neil Harvey and Bill Ponsford who played 46, 41 and 40 innings respectively before failing to score.

In the Headingley Test of June 1989 against the all-conquering Australians, England's captain David Gower became the only batsman to play 100 consecutive Test innings without a duck. As his previous duck in a Test was made

Playing his 100th Test, Allan Border is bowled by Curtly Ambrose for a duck on the MCG on 26 December 1988. (*The Age*, Melbourne)

in August 1982, he avoided a Test duck for eight years spanning 71 Tests and 119 innings when caught in the Melbourne Test of December 1990. Allan Border's duck in his 100th Test off the Windies beanpole Curtly Ambrose's yorker on 26 December 1988 ended a sequence of 89 duck-free innings in 52 Tests and prompted an Editorial in the *Sydney Morning Herald*. Others who have played 67 or more Test innings without a duck are England's Ken Barrington (78), Lloyd (76), Herbie Taylor of South Africa (72), New Zealander Glenn Turner (69), and Wally Hammond and Geoff Boycott of England and Australia's Doug Walters (67 each).

For those playing over 50 Test innings, Clyde Walcott (West Indies) and Lindsay Hassett (Australia) have scored fewest ducks, one each, in 74 and 69 innings. The next in line are England's Herbert Sutcliffe and Australia's Colin McDonald — both dour openers — two ducks each from 84 and 83 innings respectively.

Border b. Ambrose 0 in his 100th Test. Another angle.
(Shane Backx, Ken Piesse and *Cricketer* magazine)

Find the Bail Competition! Allan Border sees his stump cartwheeling. *(The Sydney Morning Herald)*

In England, John Ikin did not score a nought until his 100th first-class innings, although he did make a duck in Australia in the Brisbane Test of 1946–47, his 57th innings. Denis Compton went from June 1946 to June 1948 without a 0 in 115 consecutive innings and Hammond played 113 innings without a nought from August 1925 to June 1928.

Left-handed Australian opening batsmen seem equally adept in their duck-evading habit at first-class level. Bill Lawry played 103 innings before his first duck. This eclipsed Arthur Morris's record of 101 first-class innings before his premiere 'zilch'.

Morris attributes this aberration to his 'fatal attraction' for an Afrikaans girl. As he wrote in *The Primary Club's Middle and Leg*:

'Before the first Test at Johannesburg against South Africa in December 1949, I fell under the spell of a very lovely Afrikaans girl. As a 27-year-old bachelor, her influence on me was quite considerable, and as I went out to bat my mind was far from occupied with the job of opening Australia's innings.

'Behind me lay 101 innings in first-class cricket without a single duck but now as I shaped to face fast bowler Cuan McCarthy I was consumed by wonderful feelings of well-being I had never felt before.

'McCarthy dropped one short and I tucked my head under my left shoulder to avoid being hit, and went through what could be described as an optimistic hook shot. I missed the ball completely but it brushed my batting glove, glanced on to my shoulder and flew to Hugh Tayfield at first slip.

'There was a half-hearted appeal from fieldsmen behind the wicket. I looked up at the umpire and this was where things got out of hand. The umpire gave me not-out, but in my befuddled state of mind I walked. In my 102nd knock in big cricket I had given myself out for a duck, letting down my team and my special fan, and made a fool of the umpire. Only a man under extreme emotional stress could have been so stupid.

'That first duck of mine illustrates a message all aspiring young cricketers should learn; stay away from beautiful women before a Test match. Of course, had I been playing today, the team coach, psychologist, hypnotist, physiotherapist and those ghastly pre-match exercises would have so mentally and physically exhausted me they would have compelled me to concentrate. But in my day players were not pampered the way they are now.'

Despite all his consistency, Morris was regarded as Alec Bedser's bunny. After dismissing him in the first three Tests of the 1950–51 series in Australia for 25, 0, 2 and 0, Bedser presented him with a book, *Better Cricket* by Lindsay Hassett and Ian Johnson, on his 29th birthday with a greeting: 'I hope this will help you'.

After thanking him, Morris hit 206, his highest Test score, in their next meeting at Adelaide.

No strangers to ducks, pairs and tons, Mark Waugh and Allan Border see flying stumps and bails *(The Sydney Morning Herald)*

3 Zero Heroes

as stumps and bails fly through the air
oh! not again another pair!

— James Ward

When India's mystery spinner Bhagwat Chandrasekhar bowled, batsmen hoped for the best. Even the great Vivian Richards had problems in anticipating his turn. So did Syed Kirmani who regularly kept for him for his state, Karnataka, and for India.

But when Chandra batted, bowlers rubbed their hands in glee. Here was his chance of getting his first wicket or to convert an anonymous 4-for into a *Wisden*-recognised five wickets in an innings.

At top level Chandra is recognised as a 'zero hero'. And he did not let his supporters down when he toured Australia under Bishan Bedi in 1977–78. As a bowler he won a Test for India at Melbourne, the third in the series, with identical figures of 6 for 52 in both innings.

As a batsman also he had identical figures — of 0 and 0. Unknown to many, he had created a Test record with the bat in this match. He became the first batsman to record four pairs at Test level, following his double disasters against New Zealand in 1975–76 at Wellington, against England at Delhi in 1976–77 and against Australia in the first Test at Brisbane the following season. In fact he would have had the distinction of registering three pairs in successive Tests had he not managed to remain unbeaten in both innings of the second Test at Perth without scoring.

When Bedi declared India's first innings in the Sydney Test at 8 for 396, and India won by an innings, Chandra did not have an opportunity to add to his record. Then came the final Test at Adelaide with Chandra's scores in the series resembling a pearl necklace — 0, 0; 0*, 0*; 0, 0.

He had proven his reputation as a prototype number-11 batsman and when he came in to bat, the Adelaide spectators gave him a rousing reception. Amid cheers and whistles he scored 2 and 2 to average 0.66 in the series. To make up he had taken 28 wickets at 25.14.

Oh what a feeling! India's accomplished duckster (and world-class leg-spinner), B.S. Chandrasekhar scores his *first* run in the *final* Adelaide Test against Australia in 1978 after failing to break the duck in previous four Tests. *(The Sydney Morning Herald)*

Although Chandra will be remembered as a bewildering spinner (his polio-withered bowling arm adding to the mystery effect) he holds several Test records as a batsman — or is it a non-batsman? Amongst these are: most pairs, (4; including a King Pair when dismissed first ball in both innings); most ducks, (23); highest percentage of ducks, 56.10% (23 in 41 completed innings); and the only bowler with over 100 victims to have taken more wickets (242) than score runs (167). Chandra's batting average of 4.07 established his batting skills!

It appears that spin bowlers are adept at making ducks. Of the four top duck makers in Test cricket, three are spinners: Chandra leading with 23 ducks, his spin-partner Bedi with 20 and England's Derek Underwood with 19. Pakistan wicket-keeper Wasim Bari, the odd man out, also made 19 ducks. (For a detailed list of Test duck makers, see Appendix II).

In the incidence of ducks per completed Test innings (qualification, a minimum of 14 ducks) spinners have also dominated — grabbing the top three places: Chandra 56.10% (23 ducks in 41 completed innings), India's bespectacled spinner Dilip Doshi 50% (14 ducks in 28) and the West Indian mystery spinner, Sonny Ramadhin 31.82% (14 ducks in 44).

In zero-sequence, Bedi at one stage made eight ducks in 10 consecutive Test innings: 0, 0, 0, 14, 0, 0, 1*, 0, 0, 0 against England in 1972–73 and 1974 and against West Indies in 1974–75.

Australia's leg spinner, Bob Holland, scored most Test ducks in a row — five. In three consecutive Tests in 1985, he scored 0 and 0 (Birmingham Test v England), 0 and 0 (Brisbane Test v New Zealand) and 0 (Sydney Test v New Zealand), making it five ducks in a row without a 0 not out to spoil the effect.

Australian medium pacer Alan Hurst created a Test record when he made six ducks (with two pairs) against England in 1978–79 scoring 0 and 0, 5 and 5, 0 and 0*, 0 and 0, 17* and 13, 0 and 4. His unbeaten blob in the second innings of the third Test at Melbourne robbed him of a record three pairs in a series. He scored his third Test pair of the season against Pakistan the next month on the MCG. In all, he made 10 ducks in 12 Tests.

Fellow Victorian pace bowler Merv Hughes started his Test career with three ducks; the first one against India at Adelaide in 1985–86 and then a pair against Mike Gatting's Englishmen the next season at Brisbane. As mentioned earlier, three others started their Test career with three ducks: Tom Ward (South Africa, 1912), Bob Massie (Australia, 1972) and Brendon Bracewell (New Zealand, 1978). However, since 1989 Merv Hughes has developed his batting and can be described as a zero hero only under protest.

The Ashes series of 1903–04 in Australia established a record; 34 ducks in five Tests. Zeros were recorded by champion batsmen Victor Trumper, Monty Noble, Syd Gregory, Warwick Armstrong, George Hirst, Tom Hayward, Plum Warner and Johnny Tyldesley. This record was broken in 1978–79 in a six-Test series with 37 ducks, with Australia contributing 26 ducks — a series record for one team — to England's 11.

The following batsmen have made four consecutive ducks in Test matches:

Batsman	Team	Opponent	Series
R. Peel	England	Australia	1894–95
R.J. Crisp	South Africa	Australia	1935–36
Pankaj Roy	India	England	1952
L.S.M. Miller	New Zealand	South Africa	1953–54
W.M. Clark	Australia	India	1977–78
P.I. Pocock	England	West Indies	1984
N.R. Foster	England	Australia, West Indies	1985, 1985–86
R.G. de Alwis	Sri Lanka	India, Australia	1986–87, 1987–88
M.E. Waugh	Australia	Sri Lanka	1992–93

Of these, Peel, Crisp, Clark and Waugh each scored two consecutive pairs.

Crisp's ins and outs were so quick they could be termed instant death; he was dismissed four times in five balls.

Four Tests are remembered for the special reason that in each of them three pairs were recorded by one team.

In the Auckland Test of 1954–55 against England, New Zealanders Matt Poore, Ian Colquhoun and John Hayes made a pair each. It could have been four pairs but Alex Moir scored 0 and 0 not out. In this Test, 10 ducks were witnessed, eight of these contributed by the Kiwi bats. In the second innings, the home team collapsed for 26, the lowest total in Test history. And each of the pair-makers was dismissed by the same bowler in both innings: Poore by Frank Tyson, Colquhoun by Bob Appleyard and Hayes by Brian Statham.

In the Adelaide Test of 1974–75, Englishmen Denis Amiss, Derek Underwood and Geoff Arnold made a pair each. So did Majid Khan, Wasim Bari and Sikander Bakht for Pakistan against Australia at Perth in 1978–79. Then in the 1990–91 Chandigarh Test in India, Marvan Attapattu, Rumesh Ratnayake and Graeme Labrooy bagged pairs for Sri Lanka v India.

Five batsmen have been dismissed for pairs by the same fielding combinations. They are:

Batsman	How out	Team	Opponent	Venue	Series
R. Peel	st. Jarvis b. Turner	England	Australia	Sydney	1894–95
J. Darling	c. Braund b. Barnes	Australia	England	Sheffield	1902
P.T. Lewis	c. Woolley b. Barnes	South Africa	England	Durban	1913–14
P.G. Joshi	c. Worrell b. Valentine	India	West Indies	Bridgetown	1952–53
K.D. Mackay	c. Oakman b. Laker	Australia	England	Manchester	1956

It was Lewis' only Test appearance. The paradox is that he was picked in the first Test at Durban after hitting a brilliant 151 for Western Province against the MCC in the opening match of the 1913–14 tour. Subsequently, he severely wounded his leg in the First World War and never played first-class cricket again. By a coincidence, all the three characters in the Durban Test of 1913–14 lived to be nonagenarians; Lewis and Frank Woolley, 91 years each, and Sydney Barnes, 94.

Barnes captured 49 wickets in this four-Test series at an

astonishing average of 10.94. And 14 of his victims could not break their ducks — a series record of round dimensions!

No treatise on great bowling would be complete without the mention of Jim Laker's 19 for 90 against Australia in the Manchester Test of 1956. Eight of his victims failed to score and two of them — Neil Harvey and Ken Mackay — made pairs.

Not far behind was Pakistan's stormy petrel, Sarfraz Nawaz. In the Melbourne Test of 1979–80, he took 9 for 86 in the second innings, at one stage 7 for 1 off 33 deliveries. Set 382 to win, Australia was comfortably placed at 3 for 305 when Sarfraz started his demolition job and the hosts were shot out for 310. The Pakistani fast bowler had dismissed five Australians for ducks in the second innings.

In a Test career of controversy and devastation, England pace bowler Fred Trueman was the first to dismiss 50 batsmen for ducks, his pet victim being India's Pankaj Roy with five noughts — four times in the 1952 series alone. The record for creating maximum Test ducksters is held by New Zealand's Sir Richard Hadlee, dismissing 66 batsmen for ducks, followed by Kapil Dev 65, Imran Khan 62, Bob Willis and Malcolm Marshall 57 each, Fred Trueman 50, Ray Lindwall and Ian Botham 49 each.

Oddly, all these bowlers have been speedsters. In this group, Lindwall has the best record of 'shooting' 0.80 ducks per Test, Hadlee 0.77, Trueman 0.74, Imran Khan and Marshall 0.70 each.

Complete statistics on ducks at Test level are given in Appendix II. Interesting highlights are listed below:

On an average, 12% of batsmen dismissed in Test cricket have scored noughts. In the 1,223 Tests played before June 1993, 4,476 ducks have been recorded, the average number per Test being 3.66. Pakistani batsmen have been most adept at avoiding ducks, with only 1.60 per Test.

Thirty-four batsmen have the unmentionable average of 0 in the 116 year history of Test cricket. This includes 13 South Africans, 9 Englishmen, 6 Australians, 3 New Zealanders,

Richard Hadlee, the prolific wicket-taker and duck-inflictor in Test cricket, caps it all in this unusual headgear. He dismissed a record 66 batsmen for ducks in Test matches. (Utpal Sorkar and *Wisden Cricket Monthly*, England)

2 Indians and a lone Pakistani. Eight of them recorded pairs and 18 made ducks in their sole Test appearance.

Ducks are fairly common on Test fields and only 54 matches (4.41%) have been free of them. Surprisingly, there has not been one Test match in which all 40 wickets fell with no ducks recorded.

'I still remember the pang of making a duck,' says a grim Steve Waugh. 'I hope Kapil Dev (also in the pic) does not add me to his duck collection.'
(The Sydney Morning Herald)

4 Triumphs and Tragedies

One thing you can be sure of in cricket,
and that is, you can't be sure of anything.

There have been four instances of a batsman scoring a double century and a duck in the same Test.

Only one batsman, Dudley Nourse of South Africa, has overcome the blow of a first-innings blob with a double century in the second. It happened in the Johannesburg Test of 1935–36 when he was up against an Australian attack of Ernie McCormick, Bill O'Reilly, Clarrie Grimmett and 'Chuck' Fleetwood-Smith.

Nourse wrote in his autobiography, *Cricket in the Blood*: 'Once again I fell prey to McCormick and that for my second nought against Australia. Would there be the inevitable third? They so often go in such cycles.'

That was on Christmas Day, 1935, but the next two days were to bring him glory. In the second innings on Boxing Day he was on 96 with 20 minutes to go for stumps but could score no further. In the previous Test he was dismissed for 91, so he had a restless night and could not sleep till after 3 am. His insomnia was really unnecessary because not only did he get his first Test century but went on to record 231, which remained the highest Test score by a South African till 1951 when Eric Rowan hit 236, which is still a record innings in a Johannesburg Test.

The other three batsmen had a contrasting experience.

Arriving at the crease full of confidence with a first-innings double century under their belt, they soon discovered the meaning of anti-climax as they returned to the pavilion, amid embarrassing silence for their noughts. They are:

Batsman	Scores	Team	Opponent	Venue	Series
Imtiaz Ahmed	209 & 0	Pakistan	New Zealand	Lahore	1955–56
S.M. Nurse	201 & 0	West Indies	Australia	Bridgetown	1964–65
I.V.A. Richards	208 & 0	West Indies	Australia	Melbourne	1984–85

So far, 71 batsmen have scored centuries (including double hundreds) and ducks in the same Test on 79 occasions; a century and a nought 45 times, and a 0 and a century 34 times.

SUMMARY

For	Total	Aus.	Eng.	S.A.	W.I.	N.Z.	Ind.	Pak.	S.L.	Zim.
Australia	17	–	10	–	3	1	1	2	–	–
England	18	11	–	1	2	2	1	1	–	–
South Africa	6	4	1	–	1	–	–	–	–	–
West Indies	14	4	6	–	–	2	2	–	–	–
New Zealand	5	–	1	–	1	–	1	1	1	–
India	10	3	4	–	2	–	–	1	–	–
Pakistan	8	3	1	–	1	1	2	–	–	–
Sri Lanka	1	1	–	–	–	–	–	–	–	–
Zimbabwe	–	–	–	–	–	–	–	–	–	–
Total	79	26	23	1	10	6	7	5	1	–

THE COMPLETE LIST

	1st inns	2nd inns	Opponent	Venue	Series
Australia (17 instances; 16 players)					
W.L. Murdoch	0	153*	England	The Oval	1880
G.H.S. Trott	0	143	England	Lord's	1896
C. Hill	188	0	England	Melbourne	1897–98
D.G. Bradman	0	103*	England	Melbourne	1932–33
J.H.W. Fingleton	100	0	England	Brisbane	1936–37

	1st inns	2nd inns	Opponent	Venue	Series
D.G. Bradman	138	0	England	Nottingham	1948
S.G. Barnes	0	141	England	Lord's	1948
R.N. Harvey	122	0	England	Manchester	1953
I.R Redpath	0	132	West Indies	Sydney	1968–69
I.M. Chappell	138	0	India	Delhi	1969–70
I.C. Davis	105	0	Pakistan	Adelaide	1976–77
R.B. McCosker	0	105	Pakistan	Melbourne	1976–77
C.S. Serjeant	0	124	West Indies	Georgetown	1977–78
G.N. Yallop	0	114	England	Manchester	1981
G.R. Marsh	118	0	New Zealand	Auckland	1985–86
D.C. Boon	103	0	England	Adelaide	1986–87
M.E. Waugh	139*	0	West Indies	St John's	1990–91

England (18 instances; 17 players)

	1st inns	2nd inns	Opponent	Venue	Series
L.C. Braund	102	0	Australia	Sydney	1903–04
J.T. Tyldesley	0	100	Australia	Leeds	1905
G. Gunn	122*	0	Australia	Sydney	1907–08
F.E. Woolley	0	123	Australia	Sydney	1924–25
G.B. Legge	196	0	New Zealand	Auckland	1929–30
D.C.S. Compton	145*	0	Australia	Manchester	1948
L. Hutton	101	0	New Zealand	Leeds	1949
P.B.H. May	0	112	South Africa	Lord's	1955
M.C. Cowdrey	119	0	West Indies	Port-of-Spain	1959–60
D.S. Sheppard	0	113	Australia	Melbourne	1962–63
M.C. Cowdrey	101	0	West Indies	Kingston	1967–68
D.L. Amiss	158	0	Pakistan	Hyderabad	1972–73
D.W. Randall	0	150	Australia	Sydney	1978–79
I.T. Botham	0	118	Australia	Manchester	1981
G. Boycott	137	0	Australia	The Oval	1981
M.W. Gatting	100	0	Australia	Adelaide	1986–87
D.I. Gower	100	0	Australia	Melbourne	1990–91
C.C. Lewis	0	117	India	Madras	1992–93

South Africa (6 instances)

	1st inns	2nd inns	Opponent	Venue	Series
J.H. Sinclair	0	104	Australia	Cape Town	1902–03
G.A. Faulkner	122*	0	Australia	Manchester	1912
R.H. Catterall	0	120	England	Birmingham	1924
A.D. Nourse	0	231	Australia	Johannesburg	1935–36
E.J. Barlow	114	0	Australia	Brisbane	1963–64
A.C. Hudson[a]	163	0	West Indies	Bridgetown	1991–92

[a] A.C. Hudson is the first South African to hit a century in his Test debut

	1st inns	2nd inns	Opponent	Venue	Series
West Indies (14 instances; 12 players)					
I. Barrow	105	0	England	Manchester	1933
F.C.M. Alexander	0	108	Australia	Sydney	1960–61
S.M. Nurse	201	0	Australia	Bridgetown	1964–65
G.S. Sobers	0	113*	England	Kingston	1967–68
C.A. Davis	103	0	England	Lord's	1969
G.S. Sobers	132	0	India	Port-of-Spain	1970–71
A.I. Kallicharran	0	103*	India	Port-of-Spain	1975–76
R.C. Fredericks	0	138	England	Lord's	1976
D.L. Haynes	0	122	New Zealand	Christchurch	1979–80
C.L. King	0	100*	New Zealand	Christchurch	1979–80
I.V.A. Richards	0	182*	England	Bridgetown	1980–81
I.V.A. Richards	208	0	Australia	Melbourne	1984–85
R.B. Richardson	104	0	England	Birmingham	1991
K.L.T. Arthurton	157*	0	Australia	Brisbane	1992–93
New Zealand (5 instances; 4 players)					
G.T. Dowling	129	0	India	Bombay	1964–65
B.F. Hastings	0	117*	West Indies	Christchurch	1968–69
M.D. Crowe	174	0	Pakistan	Wellington	1988–89
J.G. Wright	116	0	England	Wellington	1991–92
M.D. Crowe	0	107	Sri Lanka	Colombo SSC	1992–93
India (10 instances; 9 players)					
V. Mankad	111	0	Australia	Melbourne	1947–48
Pankaj Roy	140	0	England	Bombay	1951–52
V.L. Manjrekar	133	0	England	Leeds	1952
M.L. Apte	0	163*	West Indies	Port-of-Spain	1952–53
V.L. Manjrekar	108	0	England	Madras	1963–64
G.R. Viswanth	0	137	Australia	Kanpur	1969–70
S.M. Gavaskar	0	118	Australia	Melbourne	1977–78
D.B. Vengsarkar	0	103	England	Lord's	1979
N.S. Sidhu	116	0	West Indies	Kingston	1988–89
M. Azharuddin	0	109	Pakistan	Faisalabad	1989–90

David Gower avoided a duck in 119 Test innings—a record. Here he is bowled for a nought by Richard Hadlee. *(The Sydney Morning Herald)*

The Australians are jubilant as Vivian Richards is bowled by Terry Alderman for a blob in the Melbourne Test of 1981. (Ken Piesse and *Cricketer* magazine)

Garry Sobers is ecstatic when he dismisses Indian and later Queensland allrounder Rusi Surti. (Courtesy Rusi Surti)

	1st inns	2nd inns	Opponent	Venue	Series
Pakistan (8 instances; 6 players)					
Imtiaz Ahmed	209	0	New Zealand	Lahore	1955-56
Imtiaz Ahmed	122	0	West Indies	Kingston	1957-58
Hanif Mohammad	160	0	India	Bombay	1960-61
Javed Burki	140	0	England	Dacca	1961-62
Asif Iqbal	0	152*	Australia	Adelaide	1976-77
Sadiq Mohammad	105	0	Australia	Melbourne	1976-77
Asif Iqbal	0	104	India	Faisalabad	1978-79
Ijaz Ahmed	122	0	Australia	Faisalabad	1988-89
Sri Lanka (1 instance)					
A. Ranatunga	127	0	Australia	Colombo SSC	1992-93

Australia's Billy Murdoch was the first to sample such a mixed diet; 0 and 153 not out in The Oval Test of 1880. Eight tasted it twice; Don Bradman, Imtiaz Ahmed, Vijay Manjrekar, Colin Cowdrey, Garry Sobers, Asif Iqbal, Viv Richards and Martin Crowe. India's Gundappa Viswanath and South Africa's Andrew Hudson are the only ones to do so in their Test debuts.

Eddie Barlow (South Africa) and David Gower (England) are the only batsmen to score a century, a duck and a century in successive Test innings.

Barlow hit 114 and 0 against Australia in December 1963 and 109 in the next Test on the MCG. Gower scored his 100 and 0 in the Melbourne Test against Australia in December 1990 and followed with 123 on the SCG in January 1991 in the next Test.

Vijay Manjrekar (India) made 108 and 0 against England at Madras in 1963-64, followed by another duck in the next Test at Bombay.

There have been five instances in which batsmen from opposite sides developed this 'duck century' syndrome in the same Test. They are:

Colin Cowdrey (101 & 0) and Garry Sobers (0 & 113*)
West Indies v England, Kingston, 1967-68

Ian Davis (105 & 0) and Asif Iqbal (0 & 152*)
    Australia v Pakistan, Adelaide, 1976–77
Rick McCosker (0 & 105) and Sadiq Mohammad (105 & 0)
    Australia v Pakistan, Melbourne, 1976–77
Ian Botham (0 & 118) and Graham Yallop (0 & 114)
    England v Australia, Manchester, 1981
Mike Gatting (100 & 0) and David Boon (103 & 0)
    Australia v England, Adelaide, 1986–87

India's elegant batsman, Gundappa Viswanath, started his
Test career under a cloud of self-doubt against Australia when
dismissed for a blob in the first innings of the Kanpur Test
of 1969–70. The 5'4" (160-cm), 20-year-old was consoled by
his skipper Nawab of Pataudi (jnr) who said: 'Not to worry,
Vish, you'll hit a ton in the second innings'. He did exactly
that — 137 with 25 fours against 'Garth' McKenzie, 'Alpal'
Connolly, Johnny Gleeson and 'Rowdy' Mallett.

Even ducks have their uses. Gerald Brodribb states that
Dick Barlow of Lancashire once wore down the bowling for
65 minutes before being out for a nought.

In 1946, Jack Young's 0 not out enabled Walter Robins to
put on 75 for the last wicket for MCC v Yorkshire, Robins
making all 75 of those. R.S. Machin of Cambridge University
once went in last and helped in a 10th-wicket stand of 69,
of which his contribution was a precious duck.

The most agonising wait by a man on the verge of a pair
was experienced by Godfrey Evans, the English wicket-keeper
and normally an attacking batsman. In the second innings
of the Adelaide Test in 1947, he was on nought for 97 minutes
— the longest a batsman has taken to score in first-class
cricket.

After being bowled first ball in the first innings, Evans
came to the crease 45 minutes before stumps on fourth day
with only two wickets to go and defeat looming. His partner,
Denis Compton, controlled the strike. Evans faced 20 balls
that day and could have taken a single or two but Compton
heartlessly ordered him back.

With his duck still unbroken, Evans had a restless night. After 52 run-free minutes on the final day — and that included a missed stumping chance — he scored his first run. He went on to make 10 not out in an undefeated 85-run stand. Compton scored an unbeaten 103 and the Test was drawn.

Batsmen who waited over an hour to score their first run in a Test innings are:

Batsman	Minutes	Team	Opponent	Venue	Series
T.G. Evans	97	England	Australia	Adelaide	1946–47
P.I. Pocock	82	England	West Indies	Georgetown	1967–68
J.T. Murray	74	England	Australia	Sydney	1962–63
C.G. Rackemann	72	Australia	England	Sydney	1990–91
W.L. Murdoch	70	Australia	England	Sydney	1882–83
Shuja-ud-din	65	Pakistan	Australia	Lahore	1959–60

At lower level, G. Richards (for Harrow Blues v Civil Service, 1871) batted 77 minutes without scoring.

On 20 January 1980, Vincent Hoggs batted for 87 minutes without making a run. This was for Zimbabwe-Rhodesia B v Natal B in the South African Castle Bowl first-class competition.

When playing for Surrey against Yorkshire at The Oval in 1920, Miles Howell batted for 43 minutes in complete command. He played all Yorkshire bowlers including the great Wilfred Rhodes firmly and in the middle of the bat. Yet he scored no runs.

As R.C. Robertson-Glasgow, the noted English cricket writer, told Basil Easterbrook: 'Any spectator who entered the ground at any point in that innings and failed to observe the scoreboard might reasonably have thought that Howell was in the comfortable 30s or 40s. But the ball would not pierce those fielders. And then he was run out, bravely answering a call from his rash partner. Run out nought; with the sweat pouring from his brow. As he remarked in the pavilion: "Not a run; not even a little one, dammit; and I feel as if I'd sprinted to the House of Commons and back!" '

Thus a duck could be 'large and illustrious as well as an embarrassing spasm', concluded Easterbrook.

At times a duck can provide a sense of relief. The tall Australian fast bowler Jack 'Gelignite' Gregory had a frightening bowling action, 12 outsize steps climaxed by a kangaroo leap. Enough to terrify a rookie batsman even before he delivered. Wally Hammond remembered his first encounter with 'Gelignite' Jack in 1921 when aged 18. 'Jack Gregory had cultivated a fearsome stare and gave me the treatment', wrote Hammond. 'With knees trembling and hands shaking, I was relieved when he bowled me first ball.'

Then on a badly prepared pitch at Brisbane in 1931–32, Don Bradman had problems facing Eddie Gilbert, the Aboriginal fast bowler from Queensland. So apprehensive was Bradman that he fell down twice to avoid Gilbert's fliers. He was out in the first over and later remarked, 'Luckiest duck I ever made'.

Lesser batsmen have reacted more dramatically to such rib-tickling, scalp-seeking bowling on fiery pitches. In a Players v Gentlemen match at The Oval in 1908, a batsman was so terrified of Neville Knox's furious pace and sudden bounce that he withdrew towards square leg and allowed the ball to crash into his stumps. His parting worlds were: 'Good afternoon, gentlemen. I've got a wife and family to think of'.

Similarly, a Leicestershire batsman, Haydon Smith, found Harold Larwood's pace and lift so insurmountable that he edged a ball towards the gully and started walking. When the fielder, Sam Staple, sportingly called him back saying, 'Hey, come back, I didn't catch it', the batsman kept walking saying: 'You b-b-bloody liar, you k-k-know you did!'

And now to the *final* score. Although technically not a pair, a Pakistani batsman's score in the final of Qaid-I-Azam Trophy in Karachi in 1958–59 makes tragic reading:

Abdul Aziz retired hurt 0 in the first innings and did not bat, dead, 0 in the second.

A duck can inflict pain—ask Jamie Siddons *(left)* during a
Sheffield Shield match. (Ken Piesse and *Cricketer* magazine)

5 The Elite Rabbits

Any mug with enough talent and concentration
can make a hundred. It requires the soul and
tenacity of a martyr to score nothing and to
continue to score nothing.

— Basil Easterbrook

No one can really take this record away from Peter Judge,
the Middlesex and Glamorgan fast bowler.

Against the touring Indian team at Cardiff on 11 June
1946, he recorded a pair which is unique in first-class cricket.
Due to rain, play could not start till after lunch on the last
day, with Glamorgan three wickets down against India's 376.
They lost their last seven wickets cheaply including Judge's,
who was bowled by Chandu Sarwate for a first-ball duck.

Glamorgan followed on and to compensate the spectators
for delays by rain, Judge and Glamorgan skipper, John Clay,
decided to stay at the wicket and waived the interval between
innings. Promotion failed to endow our elite rabbit Judge
with an opener's skill and the smiling Sarwate again bowled
him first ball. Thus off two successive balls within two
minutes, Judge was bowled twice for the quickest pair in first-
class cricket.

Monty Lynch's pair at Lord's in 1977 was equally
remarkable. There was no play on the first day and only five
overs could be bowled on the second, when Surrey lost a
wicket and number-3 batsman Lynch was nought not out at
stumps. On the final day, 9 August, he was dismissed without
scoring as Surrey collapsed for 49.

The imaginative Middlesex captain Mike Brearley declared at 0 for 0 after only one ball in order to get a result. Lynch was again dismissed for a duck to bag a pair before lunch. Such a 'hungry' pair without a follow-on is unique in first-class cricket.

Surrey was again skittled out for 89 and Middlesex scored the required 139 to win in only 80 minutes for an amazing nine-wicket victory.

A.J.S. Smith of Natal got a pair with a difference. Against Western Province at Durban in 1972–73, he scored two ducks while facing only one ball. After a nought in the first innings he was run out in the second innings before he had a chance to ask the umpire for a 'middle and leg'. This is on an even higher level than a King Pair. Smith would like to settle for nothing short of a Maharajah Pair!

A batsman with two surnames once scored two ducks in one innings. S.S. Schultz, who later on changed his German-sounding surname to Storey, represented England in the third ever Test, at Melbourne in 1878–79. Later, for Gentlemen of

Quack—five little ducks all in a row—during a Mercantile Mutual match, Victoria v. Western Australia on 9 October 1992. (Ken Piesse and *Cricketer* magazine)

England XI, he played Oxford University on the Christchurch ground in 1881 and was out first ball. The pitch was so bumpy that his captain, intimidated by the success of a certain fast bowler, refused to continue batting. The match was transferred to The Parks and restarted a few hours later. Schultz was given a second chance and — you guessed it right — he was again out first ball.

A similar fate awaited the flamboyant Derek Randall for Nottinghamshire against Derbyshire at Nottingham in August 1989. Adjudged l.b.w. for a duck in the first innings on a pitch considered sub-standard, the match was resumed on an adjacent pitch on the second day. But the change of pitch did not change Randall's luck. He made another duck (l.b.w. again) and the match was all over in two days — Notts winning.

The Indian touring team of 1946, besides embarrassing Judge with a pair within two minutes, applied the Indian rope trick to Lancashire wicket-keeper T.L. Brierley as well. Brierley was a good enough batsman to have hit 23 fifties, including three centuries for Glamorgan before the war, but could manage only 0 and 0, 0 and 0 against the eastern visitors that summer.

Australia's leg-spinner Jim Higgs (later to be a national selector) toured England under Ian Chappell in 1975 and did not exactly shine with the bat. He played eight matches without scoring a run on the entire tour. Not one measly single! He batted only twice and was bowled by the only ball he faced on the entire tour.

Similarly, Joseph Emile Patrick McMaster of England toured South Africa with Major Warton's team in 1888–89. In the Cape Town Test he batted at number 9, made a duck and did not bowl or take a catch. This Test of two days duration was the only time McMaster appeared in a first-class game; the shortest career span by any English cricketer.

The name of Eric Hollies is associated with cricket's most dramatic duck when his googly bowled Sir Donald Bradman for nought in the Don's farewell Test appearance at The Oval in 1948. When Sir Donald was cheered all the way back, Hollies turned to team-mate Jack Young and lamented 'Best __ ball I've bowled all season, and they're clapping him!'

However, Hollies should be remembered in his own right as an elite rabbit, having scored 271 ducks in 616 innings. One of the few who has taken more wickets than scored runs, in 25 years he scored 1,673 runs at an average of 5.01 in first-class cricket and captured 2,323 wickets at 20.94. At Test level, the same pattern is apparent: 37 runs at 5.28 and 44 wickets at 30.27 in 13 Tests.

In a 'prolific' spell of non-scoring, Hollies registered eight zeros in nine consecutive innings for Warwickshire in 1955 and 1956. However, this included a few nought not outs. But in 1956 he was dismissed five times in six successive innings without bothering the scorer.

Hollies could suffer the zero pain as well as impart it. Apart from the dismissal which robbed Bradman of maintaining his century batting average, Hollies' other noted duck victims were Neil Harvey, Don Kenyon and John Ikin. The last mentioned had played 99 consecutive innings in first-class cricket in England without tasting a duck pie when Hollies had to spoil it.

Now we pass on to 'Super Rabbit' performances — not necessarily by rabbits, as they include a Test opener, a batsman with almost 10,000 runs in first-class cricket and a player selected solely for his batting.

In the last Shell Shield match of 1985–86 New Zealander Peter Visser of Central Districts scored a single amid a feeling of disappointment by a select band of cricket followers. In the previous 12 matches (and 10 innings) he had failed to score — which included four not outs. However, he had equalled B.J. Griffith's record of 10 noughts in a row and needed just one more for a first-class record. But Visser let us perverse statisticians down by scoring a run.

The 'record' was eventually broken by M.A. Robinson in 1990 when he made 0, 0*, 0*, 0*, 0*, 0*, 0, 0, 0, 0*, 0* and 0 in 12 successive innings for Northamptonshire.

Here are the non-scoring 'sprees' of the other two batsmen, as given by Philip Bailey in *The Cricket Statistician*:

P.J. Visser (Central Districts, N.Z.) in 12 matches
1983–84	dnb, dnb
1984–85	0*, 0 and 0, dnb
1985–86	0* and 0, dnb, 0* and 0*, 0 and 0, dnb; 0 dnb and then the terminal single!

B.J. Griffiths (Northamptonshire, England) in eight matches
1974	0 and 0*, dnb, 0* and 0, 0 and 0
1976	0 and 0
1977	0, 0

Note: dnb = did not bat.   * = not out

After a few scores in 1977, Griffiths once again got into the zero-groove with 0 and 0, 0*, 0 * 0*, 0* and 0*. Thus he followed his 10 run-less sequence with seven arid innings without adding a jot to his team's total. To sum up our prize rabbit's performance from 1974 to 1978, he failed to score in 13 out of 15 innings, 14 in 16, 15 in 17, 16 in 18, 17 in 19, 18 in 22, 19 in 23 and 20 in 26 innings. It's hard to be a duck champ, however good at them you may be, there are others who are equally non-productive. In making 20 ducks in 26 consecutive innings, Griffiths is not alone, nor is he the first. Two Kentishmen beat him to it: J.C.T. Page in 1953–54 and J.N. Graham in 1973–76.

But Griffiths was the first to achieve 10 zeros in consecutive innings, followed by Visser. Seven batsmen have played nine consecutive innings without scoring. J.P. Candler of Cambridge University had an unnerving start to his first-class career when he recorded 0* and 0, 0 and 0, 0* and 0* (1894) and 0, 0*, 0 (1895) in the first six matches of his first-class career.

Another Cambridge University blue, P.L. Garlick, had an equally confidence-shattering start 90 years later when his initial six matches brought him 2 and 0, 0, 0* and 0, 0 and 0.

But at least they had other opportunities. Somerset's reserve wicket-keeper Seymour Clarke's 0 and 0, 0 and 0, 0* and 0*, 0 and 0 and 0 in 1930 remained his only first-class innings. When going through this horror patch, an Essex bowler sympathised with his unfortunate record and bowled him a long hop. Even this dismissed him!

T.W.J. Goddard of Gloucestershire followed his 0* and 0, 0* and 0, 0* and 0, 0 and 0* and 0 in 1923 with a four. Phew, what a relief!

Leicestershire's Brian Boshier broke his sequence of nine consecutive zeros (including five unbeaten ones) in 1955 with a top score of 13 not out against Lancashire at Hinkley.

Glamorgan's O.S. Wheatley thought his batting problems were sorted out when he followed his 0* and 0, and 0 with an unbeaten 15 in 1956. But his troubles had just begun as in his subsequent eight matches he failed to score in nine successive innings — although eight times he was left without a partner.

Test medium pacer Mike Selvey played 10 matches for Middlesex in 1972 without bothering the scorer in nine successive innings (seven times not out).

Eight-in-a-row non-scorers are H.D. Read (Essex, 1935); T.S. Parankusan (Madras, 1938–40); J.C.T. Page (Kent, 1953–54); A. Hurd (Essex and Cambridge University, 1958); B.S. Chandrasekhar (Indians in Australia, 1977–78) and S.P. Perryman (Warwickshire–Worcestershire, 1981–82).

Perryman hit back in his next match, smacking a six to win the match.

The above list surely looks spectacular. But is it genuine? Somehow we zero statisticians do not consider 0 not out as a failure to score. It's like including 99 not out in a list of centuries.

Philip Bailey once again comes to our rescue with an original table in *The Cricket Statistician*. A.W. Wright of

South Australia and Englishman E.G. Hartnell are the real duck champions, the super elite rabbits. In the 1905–06 season Albert Wright scored 0 and 0, 0 and 0 and 0 and 0 in his first three matches. He went on to score 242 runs at 7.58 with a highest score of 53 and took 110 wickets at 30.81.

The only other batsman to score six ducks in a row was E.G. Hartnell in the 19th century. He followed his 2 runs with a duck in 1844, four years later made two pairs and in 1850 scored a blob and a 9 for Cambridge University and Gents of Kent.

At least 18 batsmen have recorded five first-class ducks in a row and they include an Indian Test opener. (No, he is not Pankaj Roy!). Anshuman Gaekwad (Baroda), who scored 1,985 runs in 40 Tests, ended the 1971–72 season with a pair and a duck and started 1972–73 with a pair.

Another is M.A. Buss of Sussex (with nearly 10,000 runs at the first-class level) who in 1974 followed an innings of 11 with a duck in the second innings and then two pairs.

F.J. Kendall of Northamptonshire and Captain W.W. Jelf of Leicestershire were dismissed five times in a row without breaking an egg in their only first-class innings. Our heart goes out for Captain Jelf, who was played as a batsman and broke his five zeros spell by scoring six runs. Despite stimulating batting performances at lower grade, he could not convince the selectors to give him one more go.

Even without the assistance of nought not outs, our zero-kings B.J. Griffiths, P.J. Visser, P.L. Garlick and H.D. Read do well in the real list. Garlick was dismissed five times without scoring in 1984, as also 7 times out of 8 and 8 times out of 9. Griffiths had such sterile spells in 5 out of 6 innings and 6 out of 7 during 1974 to 77. Visser returned to the pavilion scoreless 5 out of 6 times from 1983 to 1985.

Not to be sneezed at was H.D. Read's arid zone when he was dismissed runless in 5 out of 6 innings, 7 out of 8, 9 out of 12, 11 out of 16 and 12 out of 18 innings in 1935.

Another contender for the elite rabbit crown is George Deyes from Yorkshire. He scored blobs in 5 out of 6 consecutive innings, 6 in 7, 7 in 8, 8 in 9, 9 in 12 and 10 in 14 in 1907.

Australia's lanky quickie Bruce Reid is not embarrassed by his consistent low scores. 'I'm in the team for my bowling,' he explains, 'and in the nets the batters bat and bowlers bowl. If you're relying on a number 11 to win the game for you, you've really lost it because of what's happened up the order.'

One can always sense the arrival of a genuine rabbit. So used to the brevity of Fred Morley's innings was Horace, the Trent Bridge groundsman's horse during the 1890s, that it is reported he sidled unobtrusively towards the roller as soon as Fred came out through the gate.

These prolific ducksters have their uses. As Jonathan Rice asks in *Wisden Cricket Monthly*: 'After all, without the duckmasters, who would make the rest of the side look good?'

You don't have to score many ducks to get a reputation. Bert Ironmonger, the Victorian left-hander who played 14 Tests for Australia as a tailender in 1920s and 1930s averaging 2.62 with the bat, was recognised for his short innings (six noughts plus four nought not outs in 21 Test innings). When his wife telephoned the Melbourne Cricket Ground for Bert, she was told that he had just gone in to bat. She coolly replied, 'I'll hang on'.

Patsy Hendren, the great English batsman, and a character, loved to tell this story. Once he sat opposite an ashen-faced railway passenger with his coat turned up and around his ears. He appeared to be in some sort of pain so the genial Hendren asked him what his trouble was. The man replied hoarsely that he had made five ducks in a row. The sad confession shocked Hendren into exclaiming: 'Good Lord! If I made five ducks in a row I'd cut my throat.' The stranger replied: 'I have'.

6 Noughts and Sundry

> A man whose wife was in hospital expecting a
> baby telephoned the maternity ward to get the
> news. By mistake he got the local cricket
> ground. When he asked about the latest
> position he was told: 'There are seven out
> already and the last two were ducks'.

Apocryphal, no doubt. All the same, the story indicates how deep ducks are in folklore.

In minor cricket, ducks are so abundant that usually a whole team has to be dismissed for nought to get a few inches of space in the local paper. Hence, what we know may only be a tip of the iceberg. On the other hand, I have been careful that a pub boast does not gate crash.

On 10 June 1974, The *Australian* and *Daily Telegraph* (Sydney) described a most unusual match. It is hard to believe, but a team in England's Huddersfield Junior League won a match in which not a single batsman scored a run.

The home team from the nearby village of Holmbridge batted first and were shot out for 1 — a wide. Their opponents, Holmfirth, scored four leg byes from the second ball of the opening over and won the match. Paul Hartley and Ashley Mills from Holmfirth were responsible for all 10 wickets and all five runs. Hartley took six wickets and Mills four; Mills bowled the wide and the leg byes came off Hartley's legs.

There is a parallel to this astounding result. Harvey Day,

an English writer specialising in minor cricket, described a low-scoring match between Bede's Central School and Mortimer Road School in North Shields in 1931. The latter were dismissed for zero and though none of the St Bede's boys could manage a single between them, they won through a sundry.

A. Dartnell of Broad Green realised the dream of all bowlers, to capture 10 for 0. He achieved this against Thornton Heath at Croydon (U.K.) in 1967 as the opponents were dismissed for nought.

George Mell presents a similar match in *This Curious Game of Cricket*. On 22 June 1952 at Bookham, Surrey, the local club dismissed the Electrical Trades Commercial Traveller's Association Cricket Club for 0. Bookham won without a run scored from the bat, the first ball streaking for four byes.

'Mr Extras' made a huge contribution in a match between Van Thyland's XI and Jaegar's Danis XI at Bognor Regis, Sussex, in 1951. The former batted first and made 102 of which S. Anderson hit two, others registered 'ducks, only ducks and nothing but ducks', while sundries contributed a round 100.

Such freaky happenings enrich minor cricket literature. The following instances of weird endings are taken from Julian Oakley's *Cricket Companion 1974* — a publication of the Canberra branch of Australian Cricket Society. A Saturday afternoon match in England on 29 June 1968 between Chaffcombe and Symene finished within an hour. The former totalled 3 in 34 balls. When Symene batted, their opener Knight hit a four off the very first ball to win the game.

In another epic finish in 1883, A.B. Holman's XII defeated F.P. Howlett's XII by an innings after leading by only one run in the first innings. To Howlett's 75, Holman's replied with 76. Then in a sensational collapse, Howlett's were all out for nought.

Mind boggling? At Midlands in England, Diseworth batted first and were dismissed for just 1 — the vicar's son being the top scorer or rather the only scorer. But they fought back, skittling out opponents Kegworth for zero.

In August 1855 the Second Royal Surrey Militia met Shillinglee in Sussex at the seat of Earl Winterton. The scorecard of the Militia's first innings was as follows:

Private Dudley	b. Challen jnr	0
Private Plumridge	b. Heather	0
E. Hartnell, Esq.	b. Heather	0
A. Marshall, Esq.	b. Challen jnr	0
Private Ayling	b. Challen jnr	0
Lieut Pontifex	b. Heather	0
Corporal Heyes	b Heather	0
Lieut Ball	b. Heather	0
Major Ridley	not out	0
Sgt Ayling	run out	0
Private Newberry	b. Heather	0
Extras		0
Total		0

No catches, no stumpings, no lbw's and no runs!

To quote Basil Easterbrook from *Wisden 1971*: 'No. 10 batsman Sgt Ayling nearly ruined the whole thing. He hit one to cover point and set off like an Olympic sprinter going for the tape. Major Ridley rent the pastoral scene with a stentorian voice of command: "Go back Sergeant." Sgt Ayling pulled up all standing, fell base over apex and was run out by 15 yards. There were those who accused the gallant Major of moral cowardice, but I see him as a man with a sense of history.'

In *The Gillette Book of Cricket and Football*, edited by Gordon Ross, two unlikely matches are outlined. In a five-a-side match in the last century both Kent and Sussex were dismissed without a run between them.

To settle their differences, two tiny villages in Fiji decided to have a communal cricket duel. Run-getting was difficult in such a 50-a-side match with fielders everywhere — on trees, roof tops, besides a slip cordon of 12 — and the batting side could muster only 1 run. The duel ended in a tie when the opponents could do no better. But not before a minor cricket record of 96 ducks in a match — give or take a half a dozen — was created!

R.C. Robertson-Glasgow, who likened noughts to pearls, was not impressed with teams dismissed en-masse for noughts. He equated this to 11 pies thrown by 11 comedians in one act.

Although Cyril Sylvester of Malden's XI did not score a duck against Chatham's XI, his patience earns him a place in this book. Malden's XI were chasing Chatham XI's total of 111. Sylvester went as an opener and was still there when the score was 9 for 111 — his individual score an unspectacular 0 not out. But with the last man in and any result possible — win, draw, tie — he tickled a ball to the leg and amid cheers won the game for his team.

J. Martison of Eastrington had the odd experience of carrying the bat without breaking his duck. This was in a match near Selby in Yorkshire in early 1920. For the opposition, Cliffe Common, one Mr Tune captured all 10 wickets without conceding a run.

A staff versus students match at Downs Preparatory School near Bristol (U.K.) in 1951 produced surprising results and many red faces. The staff had decided to make a brisk 70 or 80 and then declare so that the juniors did not get exhausted. They batted first and collapsed against 12-year-olds J. Smith and C. Wittington, losing their first 8 wickets without a run on the board and were all out for 2. The boys reached this target easily.

A hat-trick usually produces two ducksters. A triple hat-trick (nine wickets in nine balls) creates virtually a team of embarrassment and ducks. Two schoolboys have achieved this mass duck creation. For Smithfield against Alwal North in South Africa, Paul Hugo sent back nine batsmen in nine balls in 1930–31.

A 14-year-old New Zealander, Stephen Fleming, repeated this devastating feat in 1967 for Marlborough College against Bohally School in Blenheim, New Zealand. He trapped Bohally's last man in the first innings. Then in Bohally's second innings he sent back eight batsmen in his first eight ball over.

Australia's James Dowd bowled seven batsmen in seven balls for Stanislaus College, Bathurst, in 1900–01. Poor redundant fielders — and batsmen! There are several other incredible multiple hat–tricks in minor cricket but it happened once at a higher level. Harry Boyle, who played 12 Tests for Australia as a bowler, once captured seven wickets in eight balls for Australia v XVIII of Elland at Leeds in 1878.

There are occasions when a side starts well and then comes along a bowler and it is all over — kaput! *The Gillette Book of Cricket and Football* tells the story of Ron Winfield, who was given the bowling with Nottingham City Transport's score on 3 for 39. He took six wickets with his first six balls and caught the last man off the first ball of another bowler. Seven balls, seven wickets; from 3 for 39 to 39 all out — ducks quacking all over the transport system!

Ken Sobels did a Ron Winfield in Australia. On 20 November 1976, Sobels, a B-grade Muswellbrook Workers' Club cricketer from Scone in New South Wales was given the bowling with opponents Senenhoe ABC Bunman United on 4 for 74. This proved to be his last over as he took two hat-tricks; wickets off his second, third and fourth balls and off his sixth, seventh and eight deliveries. The dazed Senenhoes were bundled out without adding to their total of 74.

Another instance of instant finish was provided in a match for the inaugural Indira Gandhi Tournament in Sydney on 8 February 1987. In reply to Gujarat's 218, Karnataka were 1 for 137 with grade cricketers Dr Janardhan (74) and Dr Hans Satyan (31) in fine touch. The match was heading for an exciting finish with their score on 4 for 152, with 67 runs needed in 11 overs. But they were all out for 152, losing six wickets in six balls, Solanki claiming five of these and one was run out. Batsman number 6 was unable to get a strike and helplessly watched the duck parade from the other end.

The most dogged duck title should go to Ivan Hutchings, aged 13. He carried his bat through a completed innings for Sulton U-13 v Streatly XI. He played for 26 overs and remained 0 not out, his 10 partners making 26 runs from the other end.

Roy Webber in *Cricket Records* presents an instance of 18 ducks in an innings. In 1861 C. Absolon, an underarm trundler for the United Master Butchers, bowled 18 of the XX of the Metropolitan Cricket Club who could total only 4.

In this chapter I have so far concentrated on a team full of ducksters rather than on a champion individual. To be included here, he would have to be 'outstanding' — getting three ducks in a match, for instance. It's not impossible, three batsmen have achieved this in 14 days.

To quote Irving Rosenwater from *Cricketer: Quarterly Facts and Figures*: 'To get two ducks in a match is a misfortune; to get three, as Oscar Wilde might have said, is plain carelessness'. Then he cites the fate of W. Welsh and W. Richmond playing for XII of Bingham against Nottingham Old Club at Bingham in 1834. The arrangement was that the Binghams should have four innings to Nottingham's two; thus Welsh and Richmond could make three ducks in this match. In the return match a fortnight later on the Forest Ground, Nottingham, Horsepool (jnr) of Bingham also registered three ducks.

Breaking a duck can get expensive. J. Knowles, for Nottinghamshire against Northamptonshire in 1937, broke two bats and borrowed a third one from team-mate W.W. Keeton before breaking his duck.

Anandji Dossa, the respected Indian statistician, gives some instances of unusual ducks in All India Schools Tournament. 12 ducks were recorded for Jammu and Kashmir team in 1959-60; four batsmen (S. Manmohan, Rashid Feroze, Surinderjitsingh and Nakal Saini) bagged pairs.

The Orissa v Bihar match of 1966-67 was remarkable as nine batsmen scored ducks in Orissa's first innings. Only the openers were exempt; R. Sikdar carried his bat for 11 and A. Bose made 2. However, in the second innings, these openers were out for ducks!

Sixteen ducks were recorded in the Orissa (32 and 33) v Assam match in 1977-78. Three of the Orissa batsmen, whose first names started with 'S' (S. Mirza, S. Wrought and S. Chaudhary) got pairs.

In Australia there are at least three documented instances of teams being shot out for ducks, according to Ernest Gross — a world authority on minor cricket. These are: Marlborough v Undaunted, Sydney, 1876-77; Cole's XI v North Fitzroy United, Melbourne, 1926-27; St Barnabas v Patrician Brothers, Sydney, 1967-68 (first innings). In the second innings St Barnabas were dismissed for 2.

I have unearthed two more such instances. In 1991, a Brisbane junior team Woodbridge was all out for 0.

Malcolm Burns, Records Officer of Auburn-Lidcombe Cricket Club in Sydney, remembers a match he actually played in 1959-60. For an under-16 competition, Australian Abrasives XI were shot out for 0 in the first innings and for 1 run in the second. The *only* batsman to make a run for them was the one least capable of doing so. Collis, the sole scorer, had his ankle in plaster due to previous injury.

The opposition Fairfield High totalled 390 to win by an innings and plenty. 'I was the first batsman to be out for a duck in that game', remembered Burns, 'and, of course, the first among nine batsmen to bag a pair.'

Stephen Gibbs, the library consultant for the New South Wales Cricket Association, brought to my notice a match in which he also played. Penrith Bowling Club's innings against Springwood started on 10 December 1983 at 1 pm at Lomatia Park. Within 35 minutes and 34 balls, they were dismissed for 12 (seven making ducks). Jeff Foote took 5 for 7 in 18 balls and Gary Cumberbatch (who later played for Penrith in Sydney's second-grade competition) took 5 for 4 in 16 balls.

'The match was of fairly high standard, about third-grade Sydney competition level,' remembers Gibbs. 'The pitch was certainly not unplayable as we scored 52 before losing our first wicket. But when we [Springwood] were 2 for 58 an extraordinary thing happened; a freak sleet storm in the middle of an Australian summer!' The ground was covered with about 8 centimetres of sleet and the match had to be abandoned.

Talking of extraordinary events, reports of five wickets falling in one ball surely sounds like pub gossip after the blood alcohol level is way past 0.05. But it is well documented in *Hill Chatter* of April 1974 — a publication of the Sydney branch of Australian Cricket Society — under the heading 'Five Wickets Fell — But Only One Ball Was Bowled':

'This item came to light in the collection of the late Mr Harold Gibson, which was donated to the Australian Cricket Society in 1974.

'It was a two-day match (Saturday afternoons). At the end of the first day the batting side had lost five wickets.

'On the following Saturday one of the two not out batsmen caught the bus to Kennington instead of Kensington. He did not arrive at the ground in time to resume his innings and was ruled out by the umpire.

'One wicket had thus fallen — no ball bowled.

'The first ball of the day was a no-ball which the batsman played to mid-on and started to run. A good piece of fielding and a smart return had the batsman run out.

'Two wickets had thus fallen — no ball bowled.

'Next ball, a good one, was driven hard straight back and struck his batting partner on the head — the ball rebounded in the air and was caught — striker out.

'The poor bugger with a cracked skull was carried off.

'Four men out — one ball bowled.

'The last man in arrived at the crease but seeing there was no one to bat with, he was ruled out. Thus the fifth wicket had fallen while only one ball was bowled!'

This incredible story is ended with the words: 'This I

believe! I was there. One of the umpires.' It is signed 'Hoot' who we presume to be Mr Gibson himself.

You gain an unfair advantage (disadvantage?) to grab press publicity if your surname is Duck. In a Combined Services v Public Schools match at Lord's on 7 August 1955, the scorebook read: Shireff b. Duck 0.

In another match at Burnham, Essex, two batsmen, C. Duck and S. Duck, were dismissed for ducks.

At a higher level, on 21 December 1983 Pakistani paceman Rashid Khan bowled Peter Duck in Griffith, New South Wales. This inspired Sydney's *Daily Mirror* correspondent Dick Tucker to write an interesting feature article.

In 1974 Peter Duck was a wicket-keeper when he caught a distant cousin (surname Duck) off the bowling of his younger brother John Duck for a duck.

'It was an under-18 match for Albury against Junee', he told Tucker. 'I don't even know the Christian name of the bloke we got out except he was a relation and captained Junee.'

Peter Duck, the Albury cricketer of the year 1982, said that he and his five brothers — all cricketers — have their share of good natured ribbing.

'And I've got an uncle named Donald too', he added. 'We cop a bit of flak when the duck season comes around in March — just when the finals are being played. It makes you feel like a goose.'

7 Zero Snippets

Duck to Swan!
During a Yorkshire Senior League match in 1981, two ducks bowled to two swans. The captain of New Earswick team, John Duck and his son Stephen, bowled to Colin Swan of Todcaster and his brother Ken.

Double Duck in Stacky's Swan Song
Keith Stackpole, the dashing Australian opening batsman and now a commentator, had the despairing experience of making the dreaded pair in his Test swan song.

In his final Test appearance at Eden Park, Auckland, against New Zealand in March 1974, Stackpole was dismissed off the first ball of the match. 'The irony of it was that it was a full toss from Richard Hadlee!' 'Stacky' remembered recently.

Scorer of 2,807 runs in 43 Tests (with a highest score of 207), Stackpole also made a nought in the second innings and never played another Test. His consolation was that 10 ducks were registered in this Test, including one by Greg Chappell. Despite Stackpole's double disaster Australia won by 297 runs on the third day.

Miller was Different
When Australia amassed 721 runs in a day against Essex in

1948, Keith Miller, 'always the man for a crisis', scored a zero
— bowled first ball!

Little by Little

The Little family of Gamblesby village gave Bill Mossop of
Penrith's third XI an unusual hat-trick. In an Eden Valley
League match, Mossop clean bowled Norman Little and his
nephews Ian and David Little off successive balls for noughts.
Later Mossop trapped John Little lbw to complete the family
downfall, reported *Cricketer* (England) of November 1974.

Century ... 15 Ducks ... Century

Bob Radford, the Chief Executive of the New South Wales
Cricket Association, has more than a nodding experience with
ducks. In an interview with Jack Egan in his book *Extra
Cover*, Radford remembers: 'I was a batsman, later an
opening batsman. I played a few seasons with North Sydney
in second and third grade, then I went to shire cricket with
Lane Cove...I scored a few runs and quite a few ducks. In
fact, I think I hold the record for most consecutive ducks
in the club. I think it's five but the stories have gone as high
as 15. They reckoned they had to be pretty quick to see me
bat!

'What happened was interesting. I scored a pretty good
hundred before the trot and then I got the five or seven or
15 or whatever it was ducks in a row. And then I got another
pretty good hundred at the end of it all. That's the way cricket
goes, isn't it?'

Oh Brother!

July 19, 1990 was a day to forget for two pairs of brothers
playing county cricket. Both Chris and Graham Cowdrey were
dismissed by Curtly Ambrose for ducks when representing
Kent v Northants at Northampton.

Worse awaited Alan and Colin Wells the same day. For
Sussex v Surrey at Guildford both collected first-ball ducks.

Lordly Duck

The donor of Sheffield Shield, Lord Henry North Holroyd Sheffield, was noted more for his love of the game than his talent. He bagged a pair in the only important match he played, for the Gentleman of Sussex against the Gentlemen of Kent in 1856.

Five Ducks all in a Row

In a John Player League match at The Oval in May 1978 against Surrey, the first five Sussex batsmen (J.R.T. Barclay, G.D. Mendis, Imran Khan, J.L. Groome and P.W.G. Parker) recorded ducks as they lost 4-0 and 6-4, D.J. Thomas claiming four of the ducksters. Back in 1872, Surrey blitzed MCC's first seven batsmen — including W.G. Grace — for nought.

Ducks in Limited Over Internationals

Pakistan created a record of six ducks in an innings in a limited-overs international. Against England at Edgbaston, Birmingham, on 25 May 1987 they collapsed from 3 for 168 in the 44th over to 9 for 178 in the 48th. At one stage they lost five wickets for two runs in 18 balls, to zoom down from 3 for 168 to 8 for 170. The zero heroes of the innings were opener Mudassar Nazar (out first ball from Greg Thomas), Number 3 bat Mansoor Akhtar (out fourth ball from Thomas) and Pakistan was two down without a run.

But after a good recovery, Mansoor Elahi, Salim Yousuf, Wasim Akram and Tauseef Ahmed were dismissed for ducks, all four falling with the total unchanged at 170. Then a 35 run last-wicket stand enabled Pakistan to reach 213. England won in the last over by one wicket in an engrossing climax.

On 25 February 1993, Pakistan equalled their unenviable record of six ducks when bowled out for 43 — the lowest score in a limited over international — against West Indies in Cape Town.

Before this, the record number of ducks in a limited over international innings was held by England (five ducks). This was against the West Indies in the second World Cup Final on 23 June 1979. England was then savaged by Joel Garner, whose deadly spell of 5 wickets for 4 runs in 11 balls shattered England from a comfortable 2 for 183 to 194 all out.

Nothing to Laugh at

Getting a duck in cricket is embarrassing enough. So imagine the plight of English cricketer David Pritchard, who was knocked out on the way to the wicket when the number '0' blew off the scoreboard and hit him on the head.

Foot and Run

According to Greg Growden in the *Sydney Morning Herald*: 'It is timely to record the more unluckier participants of this strange game such as the Sydney University third-grade opening bowler, Max Bonnell. His first seven innings in 1988 were 0,0,0,0,0,0 not out and 0. All his dismissals were bowled. But he literally broke his duck against Petersham-Marrickville in his first game in second grade when he was given a run, even though the ball came off his foot and not his bat. The second grade captain then promptly declared. Currently, Bonnell is odds-on winning the club's lowest aggregate of the season award — which means skulling a jug of beer at the annual dinner. His only opponent is veteran James Rodgers who won last season's award after tallying only three runs'.

Donald's Duck Saves Lives

So depressed was a Tasmanian, Mr Hancock, on hearing on radio about Bradman's duck in the Melbourne Test of 1932–33 that he went for a walk on the beach to cool down. As he was walking in gloom, he heard screams from a few three year-olds who were drowning. Hancock dived in his three-piece suit and rescued them.

A Six and a Duck in One Ball

Percy Fender hit a six and a duck off the same ball for MCC v. Ballarat XI at Ballarat in 1921. His huge six cleared the Ebden Street fence of the Eastern Oval, landed in a fowlyard and killed a duck.

Duck b. Gander

When Gwydir played Cripple Creek in Moree (New South Wales), Gwydir's G. Duck was bowled by T. Gander of Cripple Creek. No, he did not make a duck. He got 2. (From *Moree Champion*, November 1992).

Three 'Goldens' in Eight Days

A capable first-grade batsman, Glenn Bellamy, 22, went through a horror patch for the Wallsend Cricket Club in Sandgate, New South Wales. He made three 'golden' ducks in successive innings in eight days in February 1993. His first 'golden' came on a Sunday for an Under-23 team. His second first ball duck was in a first-grade competition run by the Newcastle District Cricket Association. His captain tried to lift Glenn's morale by promoting him to open the Under-23s innings. You guessed it; he was out first-ball.

He came good in the final though, topscoring with 40 in 99 minutes off 76 balls.

Golden Kiwis

Two opening batsmen were dismissed first ball three times during a Shell Trophy match in New Zealand in 1988–89. Opening the batting for Northern Districts against Wellington at Morrinsville, Lindsay Croker was dismissed by the first ball in the match. He completed a King Pair — out first ball in the second innings. In between, Wellington opener Graham Burnett was out first ball.

Hampshire's Rags-to-Riches Story

Hampshire was dismissed for 15 against Warwickshire at Birmingham in 1922; eight batsmen failing to score. Forced to follow-on, Hampshire amassed 521 and won by 155 runs.

Aussie Duck Parade

Victorian fast bowler Tom Antill recorded Australia's first ever duck in first-class cricket. In this pioneering match for Victoria against Tasmania on the Launceston Racecourse on

11 February 1851, he scored 0 and 0 not out. He made up for his lack of runs by taking 13 for 52 in his only match.

John Watson recorded the first pair in Australian first-class cricket when opening Tasmania's innings against Victoria on South Yarra Ground, Melbourne in March 1852. Like Antill, he was never chosen again.

Twelve ducks 'paraded' in the first ever match between New South Wales and Victoria on the MCG in March 1856; New South Wales contributing 8 ducks to Victoria's 4. In their return 'grudge' match in Sydney next season, the visitors recorded 9 ducks to New South Wales's 4. Both matches were won by New South Wales; in none of the eight innings, a team score of 100 was registered.

In the Manchester Test of 1888, eight Australians made noughts — including the first four in the second innings as Aussies tumbled to 6 for 7. In the shortest Test ever, Australia lost by an innings before lunch on the second day.

The Duck's Egg

Written on the shell of a duck's egg and found on the cricket field of Amersham Hall, on 17 July, 1886, after a match

> Two balls I survived,
>   But the third one came straight,
> For the Bowler contrived
> (Seeing what I survived)
> To bowl at a rate
>   I did not contemplate.
> Two balls I survived,
>   But the third one came straight.

Anon

8 There *is* Life After Ducks

Without the duckmasters, who would make
the rest of the side look good?
— Jonathan Rice

Except to the victim, there is something irresistibly comical about a batsman making a duck. It brings out the basic trait in human nature to laugh at others' misfortune — like a public figure caught with his pants down or dropping his dentures while making a speech, or a model losing her wig while parading.

All the batsman wants then is a big hole in the ground in which to bury himself. He shouldn't. According to William McNeill, 'without the possibility of failure all human achievements would be savourless'.

Ray Robinson, the popular Australian cricket writer and an inspiration to all around him, put ducks in perspective in his book *From the Boundary*: 'The ignominy attached to making a duck at cricket is out of proportion to the offence. By rights, it is far worse to get out for one, two or three; here go batsmen who have failed after having a look at the bowler, a sight of the ball and a feel of the wicket. Yet they walk away unshamed, whereas the man who goes for a blob first ball hardly knows where to look. As he faced the unfamiliar bowler on the unexplored pitch the only thing he could be sure of was that the Laws of Cricket specified nine ways for him to come to grief.'

R.C. Robertson-Glasgow concurred with this view. He told Basil Easterbrook: 'There are those who fancy that it is something to have scored one or two or some other disreputable and insignificant digit. They are wrong; it is nothing or, rather, worse than 0. They have but enjoyed a span too short to show a profit, long enough to show their ineptitude. They have but puttered and poked and snicked in wretched incompleteness. No; give me the man who makes 0 and doesn't care. As numbers go, he has achieved nothing; but equally, because he has never started, he has left 0 unfinished.'

Irving Rosenwater's philosophy is equally thought-provoking: 'If all the best players in cricket were good enough to avoid ever getting a duck, what a boring game cricket would be'.

Dr W.G. Grace, who found failures unbearable, told many young aspirants that a player could not call himself a cricketer until he'd been out for a duck.

No batsman — great or grotesque — has escaped encountering a duck if he played sufficient number of matches. Jack Hobbs, the champion bat with most centuries (197) and runs (61,237) in first-class matches made 42 ducks. His prolific opening partner Herbert Sutcliffe scored 40 noughts, Patsy Hendren 63 (including four pairs), the masterly Wally Hammond 49 (with four pairs) and the failure-proof Don Bradman 16. The prolific Bill Ponsford made only nine ducks in 235 innings spanning 15 years and Ray Robinson called them 'as lonely as pearls in oysters and nearly as hard for statisticians to find'.

Among recognised batsmen, George Hirst (36,323 first-class runs with 60 centuries) made the most number of blobs — 106. He was also a great bowler whose name is paired with another legendary Yorkshire all-rounder, Wilfred Rhodes, and was quite a character.

At Bradford in 1912 he bowled Australia's reliable opener Warren Bardsley for a duck. In the second innings he sent a full toss to a nervous, on-pair Bardsley who drove it for three. When thanked for this gesture, Hirst replied: 'Don't thank me, laad: it wasn't intentional'. Bardsley was overwhelmed and could score no further.

Bardsley's first-ball duck in the 1926 Leeds Test against England led to Charles Macartney recording a magnificent century before lunch. Paradoxically, Macartney was dropped fourth ball before he had scored. Keith Stackpole 'boastfully' remembers that he is only the second Australian — after Bardsley — to record a first-ball Test duck (v New Zealand, Auckland, 1974).

Very few of the cricketing greats have avoided pairs. When Ray Robinson asked Hobbs about this he replied: 'No. Towards the end of my career it was the one thing I wished to avoid.'

Among others who have avoided the 'pair of spectacles' were W.G. Grace, Ranji, H. Sutcliffe, Duleep, Herbie Taylor of South Africa, Bardsley, Compton, Macartney and Bradman. But Bradman came close to it in the Adelaide Test of 1946–47. In the first innings, the giant Surrey bowler, Alec Bedser (whom Bradman ranks as the best medium-pacer he faced in his career), bowled him for a duck. For one breathless moment in the second innings the great Don hung on the brink of a pair when facing Norman Yardley. The second ball came up against his body and cannoned back past the stumps to the wicket-keeper. It could just easily have hit them. Bradman went on to score 56 not out.

Of Don's 16 ducks, six were off first ball and three off second. Curiously, he made 0 more often than any other individual score. Next came 5 eight times. His ducks made headlines. Of his seven ducks in Test matches, three have become part of cricket history. No-one present on the Melbourne Cricket Ground on 30 December 1932 can forget his walk to the wicket in the first innings of the Bodyline Test series.

After being cheered by over 63,000 from the pavilion to the crease, Bradman dragged the first ball from Bill Bowes into his stumps and walked back in stunned silence. It was the only Test wicket Bill Bowes ever took in Australia. Jack

Don Bradman bowled for a duck by Bill Bowes in the
Bodyline series 1932–33 in front of over 63,000 Melbourne
spectators 'who refused to believe what their eyes had seen'.
(Jack Pollard collection)

Perhaps the most famous duck of all. Don Bradman bowled by Eric Hollies for nought in his final Test at The Oval in 1948. (Jack Pollard collection)

Fingleton describes this exit as 'an unbelievable hush of calamity, for men refused to believe what their eyes had seen'.

Alec Bedser is the only player to dismiss Bradman twice for ducks in first-class cricket — oddly both times in a Test match. The first time was at the Adelaide Oval on 1 February 1947. The next day cartoonist Roy Ullyett depicted the fallen hero underneath a huge baggy cap, dragging his bat through a large rounded egg, with the caption: 'It can happen in the very best circles!'

Now to the final Test at The Oval on 16 August 1948, the Don's farewell to Test cricket. After a first wicket stand of 117, entered Bradman amid unprecedented expectations. As commentators speculated on the run-machine maintaining his average of 100, he was bowled by a well disguised googly from Eric Hollies for a second-ball duck. Tossing his head back and flashing a quick smile — his usual habit of greeting his dismissal — he disappeared from Test scene with a batting average of 99.94.

Sir Donald's ducks kept cartoonists busy besides giving hopes to lesser batsmen. Another great Australian batsman and Bradman's team-mate, Stan McCabe, was a source of inspiration to others. He would pacify young batsmen dismissed for a low score by explaining that he had made a duck in his first match for St Joseph's College in Sydney, a duck in his first game for the Mosman club and a duck in his first innings for New South Wales. In his Test debut, he hit a four off the first ball. Just as well. He was dismissed next ball.

As mentioned in an earlier chapter, Len Hutton had an equally shattering start at all levels of cricket but finished as a legend. Once he scored three ducks in a row. Ironically it came in the middle of his record-breaking batting of June 1949 when he amassed 1,294 runs. No-one has scored more runs in a calendar month.

Similarly, Denis Compton had a disastrous sequence in 1946 in which he scored 0, 0, 8 and 0, 1, 0 in consecutive first-class innings. But then came 1947, his finest season, when he scored a record 3,816 runs at an average of 90.85.

Making ducks or pairs affects batsmen in different ways. England's left-handed batsman Roy Kilner was so dejected after a pair that he went home to his grandfather clock which Yorkshire had presented him and screwed off the presentation plate.

On the contrary, a pair in the Lord's Test of 1981 fired up Ian Botham to such an extent that he resigned as England's captain — hours before he could be sacked — and then hammered 50 and a scintillating 149 not out in the next Test at Leeds. It was an amazing match in which England picked itself from the ignominy of a follow-on to record a famous triumph over a dazed Australia.

Likewise, when 24 year-old Rob Eastburn of Heinz-Dandenong recorded a duck in a lower division match in Melbourne on 18 February 1984 he screamed for revenge. His opponents, Cranbourne Club, did not know what hit them the next Saturday when Eastburn belted 27 sixes and 28 fours to score 313 not out in 150 minutes. He was 'caught' twice by a wicket-keeper on the adjacent ground! He hit a six each to reach 50, 100, 150, 200, 250 and 300. He was not even tired; he had run only 39 times.

Steve O'Shaughnessy, the former Lancashire and Worcestershire all-rounder, had a contrasting experience in June 1990. He hit six sixes in an over for Saddleworth and District League club Austerlands against Droylsden. A few days later he came down to earth with a pair in his debut for Northumberland.

'Alan, my boy, there's always next Saturday', was the advice Alan Barnes, the long-serving Secretary of the Australian Cricket Board, had received from his father when in 1930 he scored three ducks in a row for Mosman's third-grade XI. He continued playing and although he did not reach first-class status on the field, his optimism for 'better luck next Saturday' helped him see through difficult times of ACB decision-making.

That, in the final reckoning, is what cricket is all about; not always shining out but hoping for success when luck is down. Often humour helps to lift the gloom of no-scores.

Lindsay Hassett was there when anyone needed cheering — even opponents. He was the skipper of Victoria in 1947–48 when he presented India's captain, Lala Amarnath (who had scored a sparkling 228 not out), with a bat autographed by his team. But he did not forget the lesser heroes. He presented Vinoo Mankad, Vijay Hazare, Khandu Rangnekar and C.R. Rangachari a celluloid duck each to mark their combined contribution of nought.

Writes Hazare in *My Story*: 'Fortunately the toy did not carry any ill omen for me in later matches and I still have it in my possession'. One of his great achievements was scoring twin centuries in the Adelaide Test a month later against the fury of Ray Lindwall and Keith Miller.

Not so for Peter May, the England captain. During his

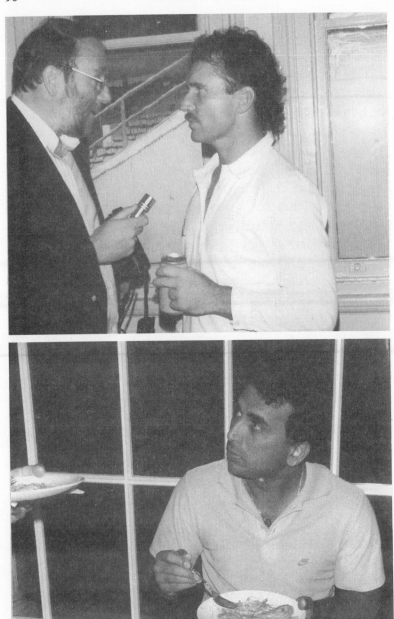

Only batsmen to top 10,000 runs in Test history, Allan Border and Sunil Gavaskar were not immune to ducks. Border *(top left)* talks 'turkey' with an English journalist while Gavaskar *(below)* gorges probably on a duck leg.

South African tour in 1956–57 he was presented with a live duck after a nought in one of the matches. Thereafter it was a struggle for the master strokeplayer to get any runs and he returned from the tour a dejected, disillusioned man.

Another Victorian skipper, Hans Ebeling — later responsible for the organisation of the Melbourne Centenary Test of 1977 — presented English opening batsman, Eroll Holmes with a cigarette lighter in the shape of a duck. This was to remind the visitor of the number of times he had scored ducks (or near ducks) off his bowling in Australia in 1935.

This book neither ridicules the ducksters nor glorifies their non-deeds. The zero heroes and elite rabbits have shone out in other departments of the game. Even for champion batsmen, scoring a few ducks is like having measles or acne — they have to go through it. And it is a consoling thought that no cricketer, however great, has had a duck-free career.

For the true philosophy of the duck, let us echo Robertson-Glasgow's sentiments: 'The essence, the aristocracy of 0 is that it should be surrounded by large scores, that it should resemble the little silent bread-winner in a bus full of fat, noisy women. Indeed, when the years have fixed it in its place, so far from being merely the foil to jewels, it should itself grow, in the fond eye of memory, to the shape and stature of a gem.'

Appendix I

The Primary Club of Australia

Out of evil cometh good.

To be dismissed first ball, referred to as getting a 'golden duck' or a 'primary', can be a shattering experience. But it has helped to raise funds for charity, to enable the disabled to play sports.

The Beckenham Cricket Club in Kent, was the first to get the idea to form a club of those players who had been out first ball. They called it the Primary Club.

Peter Howarth, a Sydney cricketer and cricket enthusiast, and John Erby, a former Sydney grade player and captain of the Sydney University Cricket Club, decided to promote the idea of a similar club in Australia. Its goal was to provide better sporting and recreational facilities for the disabled. An inaugural meeting was held in February 1974 to pursue this idea.

A committee was appointed with John Erby as president, the New South Wales Governor Sir Roden Cutler as its 'Twelfth Man' and a few cricketers including Test and state players. They were committed to involve themselves in this charity. From those early days the membership has spread to all parts of Australia with nearly 3,000 men and women involved in various aspects of its activities.

The club has as its aim the raising of funds by subscriptions, the holding of functions at its cricket ground known as Lemon Tree Oval at Dooralong, north of Wyong in New South Wales, and donations from individuals and public bodies who feel they would like to assist in the provision of assistance for facility for handicapped people. It also markets a number of products which not only promote the club but bring together a camaraderie of those people who have distinguished themselves with a 'Primary' on the cricket field.

Over the years the club has been successful in organising many functions, the reunion of the 1948 Australian cricket team being one of their most significant. They have also organised such activities as the Bodyline Ball, the Olympic Gold Medallists' Dinner and a Rugby Luncheon to honour the victorious Australian Wallabies following their tour of England in 1984.

Each year a match is played at the club's ground between the 12th Man's XI and the President's XI and people travel lengthy distances to watch the game which includes current and former Test and state players, many of whom are members of the club.

Almost a million dollars have been raised by the Primary Club of Australia. This has supported 150 registered charities. All because an Australian batsman makes a zero.

So every time your favourite batsman is out for a duck in an international match in Australia, do not despair. For such a duck involves a fine of $2 which the dedicated members of the Primary Club of Australia pay up to swell the fund.

That should take some tears off the duck's back.

Ducks in Test Cricket

(Figures accurate to 1 June, 1993)

TEAM RECORDS

Country	Tests	Ducks	Dismissals	% of ducks	Ducks per Test
Australia	524	951	8,100	11.74	1.81
England	691	1,153	10,251	11.25	1.67
South Africa	177	383	2,981	12.85	2.16
West Indies	300	538	4,461	12.06	1.79
New Zealand	219	483	3,511	13.76	2.20
India	282	530	4,271	12.41	1.88
Pakistan	206	329	2,931	11.22	1.60
Sri Lanka	43	98	688	14.24	2.28
Zimbabwe	4	11	64	17.19	2.75
Total	1,223	4,476	37,258	12.01	3.66

Note: England's 1000th duckster was P.R. Downton — v Australia at Lord's in 1985.

MOST DUCKS IN A SERIES (ONE TEAM)

Ducks	Team	Opponent	Tests	Venue	Season
26	Australia	England	6	Australia	1978–79
21	South Africa	England	5	South Africa	1913–14
21	India	Australia	5	Australia	1947–48
20	South Africa	England	5	South Africa	1935–36
20	India	England	4	England	1952
20	West Indies	England	5	England	1957

For a Three-Test Series

Ducks	Team	Opponent	Venue	Season
18	Australia	England	England	1888

MOST DUCKS IN A SERIES (BOTH TEAMS)

Ducks	Home Team	Opponent	Tests	Season
37	Australia (26)	England (11)	6	1978–79
34	Australia (16)	England (18)	5	1903–04
32	South Africa (21)	England (11)	5	1913–14
31	England (14)	Australia (17)	5	1956
31	England (15)	Australia (16)	6	1981
30	Australia (18)	West Indies (12)	5	1984–85
30	Australia (15)	West Indies (15)	5	1992–93

For a Three-Test Series

Ducks	Home Team	Opponent	Season
27	England (9)	Australia (18)	1888

FEWEST DUCKS IN A SERIES (ONE TEAM)

Ducks	Team	Opponent	Tests	Venue	Season
0	New Zealand	England	4	England	1949
1	England	South Africa	5	England	1924
1	England	Pakistan	5	England	1962
1	India	New Zealand	4	New Zealand	1967-68

For a Three-Test Series

Ducks	Team	Opponent	Venue	Season
0	Australia	South Africa	South Africa	1921–22
0	Pakistan	New Zealand	Pakistan	1964–65
0	England	India	England	1967
0	Pakistan	Sri Lanka	Pakistan	1985–86
0	Australia	India	India	1986–87
0	India	Sri Lanka	India	1986–87

FEWEST DUCKS IN A SERIES (BOTH TEAMS)

Ducks	Home team	Opponent	Tests	Season
5	Australia (3)	England (2)	4	1881–82
7	England (7)	New Zealand (0)	4	1949
7	India (3)	England (4)	5	1984–85
8	England (2)	Australia (6)	5	1926
8	India (3)	Pakistan (5)	5	1960–61
8	New Zealand (7)	India (1)	4	1967–68
8	West Indies (2)	New Zealand (6)	5	1971–72
8	Australia (3)	Pakistan (5)	5	1983–84

For a Three-Test Series

Ducks	Home Team	Opponent	Season
2	India (2)	Australia (0)	1986–87
3	Pakistan (2)	England (1)	1968–69

MOST DUCKS IN AN INNINGS

Ducks	Team (team total)	Opponent	Venue	Season
6	Pakistan (128)	West Indies	Karachi	1980–81
5	Australia (80)	England	The Oval	1888
5	Australia (70)	England	Manchester	1888
5	Australia (53)	England	Lord's	1896
5	South Africa (45)	Australia	Melbourne	1931–32
5	South Africa (390)[a]	England	Johannesburg	1938–39
5	India (277)	Australia	Adelaide	1947–48
5	India (165)	England	Leeds	1952
5	Australia (249)	England	Nottingham	1953
5	New Zealand (79)	South Africa	Johannesburg	1953–54
5	England (313)	West Indies	Bridgetown	1953–54
5	New Zealand (74)	West Indies	Dunedin	1955–56
5	England (247)	Australia	The Oval	1956
5	West Indies (146)	Pakistan	Karachi	1958–59
5	West Indies (76)[b]	Pakistan	Dacca	1958–59
5	New Zealand (79)	Pakistan	Rawalpindi	1964–65
5	England (204)	West Indies	Leeds	1976

Ducks	Team (team total)	Opponent	Venue	Season
5	New Zealand (105)	England	Christchurch	1977-78
5	Australia (310)	Pakistan	Melbourne	1978-79
5	West Indies (228)	New Zealand	Christchurch	1979-80
5	New Zealand (124)	India	Hyderabad	1988-89
5	Sri Lanka (82)	India	Chandigarh	1990-91

(a) Innings also included 5 fifties.

(b) The last six batsmen failed to score a single run between them.

Note: In India's innings of 103 v West Indies at Ahmedabad in 1983-84, six batsmen scored one run each.

MOST DUCKS IN A MATCH (ONE TEAM)

Ducks	Team (team totals)	Opponent	Venue	Season
9	Sri Lanka (82 & 198)	India	Chandigarh	1990-91
8	Australia (81 & 70)	England	Manchester	1888
8	South Africa (36 & 45)	Australia	Melbourne	1931-32
8	India (293 & 165)	England	Leeds	1952
8	New Zealand (200 & 26)	England	Auckland	1954-55
8	New Zealand (74 & 208)	West Indies	Dunedin	1955-56
8	Australia (84 & 205)	England	Manchester	1956
8	West Indies (89 & 86)	England	The Oval	1957
7	South Africa (47 & 43)	England	Cape Town	1888-89
7	England (61 & 101)	Australia	Melbourne	1903-04
7	South Africa (265 & 95)	Australia	Manchester	1912
7	West Indies (102 & 6d-51)	England	Bridgetown	1934-35
7	New Zealand (79 & 188)	South Africa	Johannesburg	1953-54
7	India (135 & 206)	Australia	Delhi	1959-60
7	New Zealand (175 & 79)	Pakistan	Rawalpindi	1964-65
7	Australia (146 & 136)	England	Leeds	1972
7	India (169 & 197)	Pakistan	Karachi	1982-83
7	New Zealand (254 & 124)	India	Hyderabad	1988-89
7	Australia (119 & 178)	West Indies	Perth	1992-93

MOST DUCKS IN A MATCH (BOTH TEAMS)

Ducks	Home team	Opponent	Venue	Season
11	England (3)	Australia (8)	Manchester	1888
11	Australia (4)	England (7)	Melbourne	1903–04
11	South Africa (5)	England (6)	Johannesburg	1913–14
11	India (6)	Australia (5)	Madras	1964–65
11	Sri Lanka (9)	India (2)	Chandigarh	1990–91
10	South Africa (6)	England (4)	Port Elizabeth	1895–96
10	Australia (4)	England (6)	Melbourne	1901–02
10	England (4)	Australia (6)	The Oval	1912
10	Australia (2)	South Africa (8)	Melbourne	1931–32
10	West Indies (7)	England (3)	Bridgetown	1934–35
10	New Zealand (8)	England (2)	Auckland	1954–55
10	New Zealand (8)	West Indies (2)	Dunedin	1955–56
10	England (2)	West Indies (8)	The Oval	1957
10	New Zealand (4)	Australia (6)	Auckland	1973–74
10	Australia (6)	England (4)	Sydney	1978–79
10	Australia (5)	West Indies (5)	Adelaide	1992–93

Note: Of 1,223 Tests played to date, 54 (4.41%) have been free of ducks, 45 of these have been drawn, seven won by Australia and one each by West Indies and England.

INSTANCES OF 30 OR MORE WICKETS FALLING IN A MATCH WITH NO DUCKS

Wickets	Team	Opponent	Venue	Series	Result
38	Australia	England	Sydney	1907–08	Australia won
38	Australia	West Indies	Melbourne	1960–61	Australia won [a]
38	England	West Indies	Nottingham	1980	West Indies won [b]
34	Australia	England	Sydney	1974–75	Australia won
33	New Zealand	Pakistan	Christchurch	1964–65	Drawn [a]
32	Australia	England	Brisbane	1958–59	Australia won [a]
30	West Indies	Australia	Georgetown	1972–73	Australia won
30	England	Australia	The Oval	1985	England won [a]

[a] One innings of 0 not out.
[b] Two innings of 0 not out.

Note: There has not yet been a Test in which all 40 wickets (or even 39 wickets) fell with no ducks being recorded.

INDIVIDUAL RECORDS

PAIR ON TEST DEBUT

Batsman	Team	Opponent	Venue	Season
G.F. Grace [a]	England	Australia	The Oval	1880
C.S. Wimble [a]	South Africa	England	Cape Town	1891–92
J.T. Willoughby	South Africa	England	Port Elizabeth	1895–96
J.J. Kotze	South Africa	Australia	Johannesburg	1902–03
P.S. Twentyman-Jones [a]	South Africa	Australia	Cape Town	1902–03
T.A. Ward	South Africa	Australia	Manchester	1912
P.T. Lewis [a]	South Africa	England	Durban	1913–14
C.D. Dixon [a]	South Africa	England	Johannesburg	1913–14
K.C. James	New Zealand	England	Christchurch	1929–30
F.T. Badcock	New Zealand	England	Christchurch	1929–30
C.I.J. Smith	England	West Indies	Bridgetown	1934–35
C.G. Rowe [a]	New Zealand	Australia	Wellington	1945–46
L.A. Butterfield [a]	New Zealand	Australia	Wellington	1945–46
C.N. McCarthy	South Africa	England	Durban	1948–49
A.L. Valentine	West Indies	England	Manchester	1950
G.S. Ramchand	India	England	Leeds	1952
G.A. Gooch	England	Australia	Birmingham	1975
B.P. Bracewell	New Zealand	England	The Oval	1978
M.R. Whitney	Australia	England	Manchester	1981
Maninder Singh	India	Pakistan	Karachi	1982–83
K.R. Rutherford	New Zealand	West Indies	Port-of-Spain	1984–85
C.M. Kuggeleijn	New Zealand	India	Hyderabad	1988–89
R. Patel [a]	India	New Zealand	Bombay	1988–89
Saeed Anwar [a]	Pakistan	West Indies	Faisalabad	1990–91
A.A. Donald	South Africa	West Indies	Bridgetown	1991–92

[a] Only Test played.

Note: For T.A. Ward it was a King Pair, dismissed first ball in both innings.

PAIR BY TEST CAPTAINS

Captain	Team	Opponent	Venue	Season
J. Darling	Australia	England	Sheffield	1902
L.J. Tancred	South Africa	England	The Oval	1912
V.S. Hazare	India	England	Kanpur	1951-52
H.B. Cave	New Zealand	West Indies	Dunedin	1955-56
F.M.M. Worrell	West Indies	Australia	Melbourne	1960-61
R. Benaud	Australia	England	Leeds	1961
Imtiaz Ahmed	Pakistan	England	Dacca	1961-62
B.S. Bedi	India	England	Delhi	1976-77
I.T. Botham	England	Australia	Lord's	1981
A.R. Border	Australia	West Indies	Perth	1992-93

Note: B.S. Bedi is the only non-batsman; I.T. Botham's pair was in his last Test as captain.

PAIRS IN TEST CRICKET

Country	Batsmen	Pairs
Australia	53	62
England	40	49
South Africa	24	27
West Indies	29	34
New Zealand	33	36
India	22	29
Pakistan	17	17
Sri Lanka	7	7
Zimbabwe	1	1
Total	226	262

Note: D.M. Jones (Australia) became the 200th player to score Test cricket's 231st pair, Australia v Pakistan, third Test, Lahore, 1988-89.

BATSMEN DISMISSED FOR A PAIR

Four Times: B.S. Chandrasekhar (India)

Three Times: R. Peel (England) [a]
R.W. Blair (New Zealand)
D.L. Underwood (England)
B.S. Bedi (India)
A.G. Hurst (Australia)
C.E.L. Ambrose (West Indies)

Twice: *Australia*: K.D. Mackay, G.D. McKenzie, J.W.
Gleeson, W.M. Clark [a], R.M. Hogg, R.G.
Holland [a] and M.E. Waugh [a]
England: A.V. Bedser, D.L. Amiss, P.I.
Pocock [a], N.A. Foster and D.E. Malcolm

South Africa: L.J. Tancred, Q. McMillan and
R.J. Crisp [a]
West Indies: C.A. Roach, A.L. Valentine and
A.I. Kallicharran
New Zealand: D.K. Morrison
India: M. Amarnath and Maninder Singh [b]

Once: *Australia*: P.S. McDonnell, T.W. Garrett, E.
Evans, F.G. McShane, A.C. Bannerman, M.A.
Noble, S.E. Gregory, C.E. McLeod, J. Darling,
J.J. Kelly, H. Trumble, V.T. Trumper, J.V.
Saunders, C.V. Grimmett, W.A.S. Oldfield,
J.H.W. Fingleton, V.Y. Richardson, C.L.
Badcock, I.W. Johnson, J. Moroney, J.B.
Iverson, L.V. Maddocks, R.N. Harvey, A.T.W.
Grout, R. Benaud, A.N. Connolly, R. Edwards,
K.R. Stackpole, G. Dymock, R.W. Marsh, J.R.
Thomson, C.S. Serjeant, A.L. Mann, D.W.
Hookes, G.M. Wood, M.R. Whitney, B.
Yardley, R.J. Bright, C.G. Rackemann, K.J.
Hughes, M.G. Hughes, D.M. Jones, I.A. Healy,
A.R. Border and J.L. Langer.

England: G.F. Grace [b], W. Attewell, G.A. Lohmann, E.G. Arnold, A.E. Knight, E.G. Hayes, M.C. Bird, H. Strudwick, P. Holmes, C.I.J. Smith, J.T. Ikin, J.J. Warr, F. Ridgeway, R.T. Spooner, J.H. Wardle, F.S. Trueman, T.E. Bailey, G. Pullar, M.J.K. Smith, J.T. Murray, B.W. Luckhurst, A.P.E. Knott, G.G. Arnold, G.A. Gooch [b], A. Ward, J.C. Balderstone, M. Hendrick, R.A. Woolmer, I.T. Botham, E.E. Hemmings, N.G. Cowans, D.J. Capel, W. Larkins and D.E. Malcolm.

South Africa: C.S. Wimble, J.T. Willoughby, J.J. Kotze, P.S.T. Jones, A.E.E. Vogler, TA Ward, CB Llewellyn, PT Lewis, J.L. Cox, C.D. Dixon, G.A.L. Hearne, A.E. Hall, F. Nicholson, X.C. Balaskas, C.N. McCarthy, D.J. McGlew, W.R. Endean, P.S. Heine, C. Wesley, M.A. Seymour and A.A. Donald [b].

West Indies: C.R. Browne, H.C. Griffith, E.E. Achong, J. Trim, A.P. Binns, O.G. Smith, S. Ramadhin, E.D. Weekes, F.C.M. Alexander, L.R. Gibbs, F.M.M. Worrell, J.S. Solomon, J.L. Hendriks, W.W. Hall, D.L. Murray, C.G. Greenidge, J. Garner, D.A. Murray, A.L. Logie, M.A. Holding, P.J.L. Dujon, A.H. Gray, K.L.T. Arthurton, D. Williams and J.R. Murray.

New Zealand: K.C. James, F.T. Badcock, J. Cowie, C.G. Rowe, L.A. Butterfield, L.S.M. Miller, M.B. Poore, I.A. Colquhoun, J.A. Hayes, A.R. MacGibbon, H.B. Cave, N.S. Harford, R.C. Motz, M.J.F. Shrimpton, A.E. Dick, G.A. Bartlett, T.W. Jarvis, W.K. Lees, B.P. Bracewell, B.L. Cairns, B.A. Edgar, G.B. Troup, J.V. Coney, I.D.S. Smith, J.G. Bracewell, K.R. Rutherford [b], J.G. Wright, C.M. Kuggeleijn [b], M.C. Snedden, B.R. Hartland and M.L. Su'a.

India: V.S. Hazare, G.S. Ramchand, Pankaj Roy, P.G. Joshi, C.V. Gadkari, N.S. Tamhane, R. Surendranath, R.B. Desai, D.N. Sardesai, M.L. Jaisimha, E.A.S. Prasanna, F.M. Engineer, D.B. Vengsarkar, Yashpal Sharma, R.M.H. Binny, D.R. Doshi, S. Venkataraghavan and R. Patel [b].

Pakistan: M.E.Z. Ghazali [c], Nasim-ul-Ghani, Wazir Mohammad, Imtiaz Ahmed, Javed Burki, Salim Altaf, Iqbal Qasim, Majid Khan, Wasim Bari, Sikander Bakht, Mudassar Nazar, Wasim Akram, Waqar Younis, Saeed Anwar [b], Aaqib Javed and Aamir Sohail.

Sri Lanka: B.R. Jurangpathy, R.G. De Alwis, M.S. Attapattu, R.J. Ratnayake, G.F. Labrooy, A. Ranatunga, S.D. Anurasiri.

Zimbabwe: D.H. Brain.

[a] Includes pairs in consecutive Tests
[b] Includes a pair on debut.
[c] Ghazali's pair was the quickest in Test cricket: it took him only 120 minutes from the start of his first innings to his dismissal in the second.

LEADING DUCK MAKERS

Ducks	Batsman	Tests	Total Dismissals	% ducks	Runs	Batting Average	H.S.
23	B.S. Chandrasekhar (India)	58	41	56.10	167	4.07	22
20	B.S. Bedi (India)	67	73	27.40	656	8.99	50
19	D.L. Underwood (England)	86	81	23.46	937	11.57	45*
19	Wasim Bari (Pakistan)	81	86	22.09	1,366	15.89	85
17	J. Garner (West Indies)	58	54	31.48	672	12.44	60
17	J.A. Snow (England)	49	57	29.82	772	13.54	73
17	T.G. Evans (England)	91	119	14.28	2,439	20.49	104
16	J.E. Emburey (England)	60	71	22.53	1,540	21.69	75
16	Kapil Dev (India)	124	164	9.75	5,069	30.91	163
15	G.D. McKenzie (Australia)	60	77	19.48	945	12.27	76

Ducks	Batsman	Tests	Total Dismissals	% ducks	Runs	Batting Average	H.S.
15	E.A.S. Prasanna (India)	49	64	23.44	734	11.48	37
15	M.A. Holding (West Indies)	60	66	22.73	910	13.79	73
15	L.R. Gibbs (West Indies)	79	70	21.43	488	6.97	25
15	D.B. Vengsarkar (India)	116	163	9.20	6,868	42.13	166
14	D.R. Doshi (India)	33	28	50.00	129	4.61	20
14	S. Ramadhin (West Indies)	43	44	31.82	361	8.20	44
14	R.M. Hogg (Australia)	38	45	31.11	439	9.76	52
14	J.R. Thomson (Australia)	51	53	26.41	679	12.81	49
14	D.W. Randall (England)	47	74	18.92	2,470	33.38	175
14	Pankaj Roy (India)	43	75	18.67	2,442	32.56	173
14	I.T. Botham (England)	102	155	9.03	5,200	33.54	208

Note: The list includes recognised batsmen — D.W. Randall, D.B. Vengsarkar, I.T. Botham, Pankaj Roy, Kapil Dev and T.G. Evans.

Among quality batsmen to make 13 ducks in Test cricket are F.E. Woolley (England) and C.G. Borde (India).

B.S. Bedi made eight ducks in 10 consecutive Test innings: 0,0,0,14,0,0,1*,0,0,0 (India v England, 1972-73, 1974 and v. West Indies 1974-75).

MOST CONSECUTIVE DUCKS

	Batsman	Team	Opponents	Series
Five:	R.G. Holland	Australia	England, New Zealand	1985, 1985-86
Four:	R. Peel	England	Australia	1894-95
	R.J. Crisp	South Africa	England	1935-36
	Pankaj Roy	India	England	1952
	L.S.M. Miller	New Zealand	South Africa	1953-54
	W.M. Clark	Australia	West Indies	1977-78
	P.I. Pocock	England	West Indies	1984
	N.A. Foster	England	Australia, West Indies	1985, 1985-86
	R.G. De Alwis	Sri Lanka	India, Australia	1986-87, 1987-88
	M.E. Waugh	Australia	Sri Lanka	1992-93

Note: J.B. Statham (England) scored 0,0*,0*,0,0,0 in consecutive innings v South Africa, Australia and South Africa in 1955, 1956 and 1956-57; B.S. Bedi made eight ducks in 10 consecutive Tests innings (see above); and R.J. Crisp was dismissed four times in five balls.

MOST DUCKS IN A SERIES

	Batsman	Team	Opponent	Series	Inn	NO	Runs	Avg
Six:	A.G. Hurst	Australia	England	1978–79	12	2	44	4.40
Five:	Pankaj Roy	India	England	1952	7	–	54	7.71
	N.A.T. Adcock	South Africa	Australia	1957–58	8	2	6	1.00
	R.C. Motz	New Zealand	South Africa	1961–62	9	1	25	3.12
	W.M. Clark	Australia	West Indies	1977–78	7	1	6	1.00
	M. Amarnath	India	West Indies	1983–84	6	–	1	0.17

DUCK IN ONLY TEST INNINGS

Batsman	Team	Opponent	Venue	Series
J.E.P. McMaster	England	South Africa	Cape Town	1888–89
G.G. Hearne	England	South Africa	Cape Town	1891–92
E.J. Tyler	England	South Africa	Cape Town	1895–96
S.D. Snooke	South Africa	England	The Oval	1907
D.W. Carr	England	Australia	The Oval	1909
R.L. Park	Australia	England	Melbourne	1920–21
W.A. Hunt	Australia	South Africa	Adelaide	1931–32
H.M. Thurlow	Australia	South Africa	Adelaide	1931–32
C.S. Marriott	England	West Indies	The Oval	1933
G.E. Bond	South Africa	England	Johannesburg	1938–39
K.D. Meuleman	Australia	New Zealand	Wellington	1945–46
S.A. Bannerjee	India	West Indies	Calcutta	1948–49
M.A. Hanley	South Africa	England	Cape Town	1948–49
I.B. Leggat	New Zealand	South Africa	Cape Town	1953–54
R.H.D. Sellers	Australia	India	Calcutta	1964–65
G.G. Hall	South Africa	England	Cape Town	1964–65
S.P. Davis	Australia	New Zealand	Wellington	1985–86
Nadeem Ghauri [a]	Pakistan	Australia	Sydney	1989–90

[a] Current player, may play more Tests.

DUCKS IN ONLY TWO INNINGS

(Excluding Pair in only Test)

Batsman	Team	Opponent	Venue	Series
D.W. White	England	Pakistan	Lahore, Karachi	1961–62
J.H. du Preez	South Africa	Australia	Johannesburg, Port Elizabeth	1966–67

OTHER BATSMEN AVERAGING 0 IN TESTS

Batsman	Team	Opponent	Venue	Series
G.A. Kempis (0, 0*)	South Africa	England	Port Elizabeth	1888–89
A.W. Mold (0, 0*, 0)	England	Australia	Lord's, The Oval, Manchester	1893
L.R. Tuckett (0, 0*)	South Africa	England	Johannesburg	1913–14
G.A. Chevalier (0, 0*)	South Africa	Australia	Cape Town	1969–70

Note: Of the 34 cricketers with a batting average of 0 in Test matches, 13 are from South Africa, 9 from England, 6 from Australia, 3 from New Zealand, 2 from India and 1 from Pakistan.

MOST DUCKS CREATED BY A BOWLER

Ducks	Bowler	Team	Tests	Ducks per Test	Wkts	Wkts per Duck
66	R.J. Hadlee	New Zealand	86	0.77	431	6.53
65	Kapil Dev	India	124	0.52	420	6.46
62	Imran Khan	Pakistan	88	0.70	362	5.84
57	R.G.D. Willis	England	90	0.63	325	5.70
57	M.D. Marshall	West Indies	81	0.70	376	6.60
50	F.S. Trueman	England	67	0.74	307	6.14
49	R.R. Lindwall	Australia	61	0.80	228	4.65
49	I.T. Botham	England	102	0.48	383	7.82

Index